On the Patio

Serving Time in a Women's Correctional Facility

Bernadette Olson Jessie
Indiana University Southeast

WAVELAND

PRESS, INC.

Long Grove, Illinois

For information about this book, contact:
Waveland Press, Inc.
4180 IL Route 83, Suite 101
Long Grove, IL 60047-9580
(847) 634-0081
info@waveland.com
www.waveland.com

To the women with whom I spent my time on the patio
and
to my brother,
whose unwavering love and support saved my life

Contents

Acknowledgments

Writing this book was far more difficult than I ever imagined. The carceral experience takes an extraordinary toll on its captives, one that reaches far beyond the prison walls. My hope is for a more compassionate and equitable criminal justice system.

I must first acknowledge the female prisoners of FCI Tallahassee, particularly those with whom I spent the most time— on the patio we cried, laughed, and loved. To the hundreds of other female inmates I met along the way, I learned a lot from our time together, and I walked out of prison with newfound insight and understanding.

None of this would have been possible without my brother, Christopher. He stood by me every step of the way. His love was the lifeline that kept me from going completely under.

I am eternally grateful for the few friends who did not cast me aside. These friendships were truly unconditional—you all loved me when I did not love myself. Your numerous letters, phone calls, and personal visits meant more to me than you could ever know.

This book would not have been possible without the help and guidance of the Convict Criminology group. Your mission of advocacy and mentoring in the lives of convicts like myself was the difference maker. I hope that I can pay forward the tolerance, kindness, and support that you demonstrated to/for me.

A very special thank you to my husband, John. I've never felt safer and more loved. You brought me back to life.

Lastly, I could not have done this without Carol Rowe, my amazing Waveland Press editor. Thank you for taking a chance on this wounded storyteller and for believing that what I had to say mattered. You gave me a forum and provided me important support and encouragement over the decade it took for me to write this book. Thank you for being my sounding board, my mentor, and my friend.

Preface

THE STORY BEHIND THE BOOK

As I began the long and arduous process of writing this book, I first sat down to contemplate the reasons why (or even whether) a need for such a book existed. I had written a prospectus of sorts for the publishers, as well as a couple of articles, but piecing together the entirety of my experiences was a challenge I was unsure I could accomplish in any real meaningful way. As I was writing the book, my thought processes and the key issues I wanted to address, changed. This book has evolved as I have evolved. Sometimes it was a purposeful addition of concrete topics such as the sexual abuse that takes place in prison or the special needs of mothers and the children they leave behind as they enter the system. At other times, memories, thoughts, or conversations would send me in another direction.

Many times, my writing of the day or week directly reflected a phone call or a letter I had received. I still maintain contact with a number of women, some of whom remain locked up and others who are in the painful process of trying to pick up the pieces of their lives after prison. I continue to be so moved by the stories these women tell—I suppose in part because I have been there—but also because I believe everyone needs to understand that the punishment of prison reaches far beyond the physical isolation of our bodies. One's mind and psyche are significantly altered after spending time with those whose work consists of nothing but breaking spirits and devaluing life.

I have changed this preface a number of times based on where I was in the writing process. And as I sat down for what I hoped was my final edit, I realized it had been almost a year since the last time I'd worked on this book. This is not to say that I haven't discussed my experiences with others, written an article to be published in some academic journal, or explained my situation to students brave enough to ask me about it. After years of procrastination, I was finally ready to finish what I had started 10 years ago. I am in an entirely different place now, both physically and emotionally. I've come to see that telling my story is less about criticizing the institutions that make up our criminal justice system, and more about the dehumanization suffered by the people defined as criminal.

I wrote this book for a number of reasons. The most important is that few people really know or care what kinds of conditions exist inside prisons, or even whether offenders live or die. It is crucial that I share my story because the atrocities of jail and prison conditions must be addressed. Policy makers, legal scholars, and justice officials continue to deny the long-term damage of even short-term incarceration, and the lifetime of labeling that comes with being a convicted felon.

I was overwhelmed and appalled by the treatment of offenders in our system. I committed a crime, and my sentence was incarceration followed by a period of probation. I have read my case files time and time again; nowhere in the files do they mention that abuse, violation, intimidation, coercion, and/or violence were part of my sentence. Policies and practices strip those convicted of committing crimes not only of freedom, but also of spirit, self-worth, and the will to live. Chuck Terry (2000), also a former convict, suggests that the effects of the criminal justice system can have a profound impact on identity. From the time of arrest to release and beyond, the forces of "correctional" systems belittle and control individuals caught within their grasps.

In my experience, as both scholar and criminal, the perspective one adopts regarding crime and punishment is based largely on agenda, ideology, and for me (and perhaps others), actual contact with those caught up in the criminal justice system. Most prison research and writing reflect the language and special interests of the prison bureaucracy. The government typically funds the studies and therefore sets the agenda, limits the parameters, and often decides if the final report will be ignored and set aside or be distributed widely and used to inform policies and procedures (Ross & Richards, 2003). I am not necessarily saying that my perspective is any better or worse simply because I have served time, but I wholeheartedly believe that those of us who have lived behind the concrete and steel barriers can better describe and shed light on our system and processes. Prison culture is unique. The demonization of the criminal offender is abetted by an overzealous media that present inaccurate portrayals of crime and criminals, self-serving political figures who have long ago realized that crime is always an election year winner, and a frightened, misinformed public—all of which contribute to a flawed and fragmented criminal justice system.

And finally, this book provides a general indictment of the criminalization and incarceration of a rapidly increasing number of women prisoners in the United States. Despite the relatively short time I spent incarcerated, I experienced and witnessed enough violence, degradation, and abuse to last me a lifetime. Punishment in the criminal justice system dehumanizes the offender in prison and beyond. Its effects are felt in all facets of our post-prison lives. There is an enduring psychological trauma produced by this experience. I have slowly come to realize that being able to speak out for convicts (and more specifically for female convicts) enables them to have voices, to resist becoming the expendable, worthless riffraff the criminal justice system says that we are.

This book is the product of my experiences; not all convicts will agree with my story or my perception, and many government workers/officials will deny or downplay the things I have witnessed and the experiences I have encountered. Additionally, I don't pretend to know how others feel, particularly those men and women who have (or will) serve inordinate amounts of time behind bars. I only ask that the reader set aside judgment, suspend preconceived notions and myths of convicts (or the system as a whole), and simply keep an open mind as I take you through my journey. This book offers a glimpse of my experiences, both into and out of the criminal justice system, a system I'd spent years being invested in, proud of, and defending.

I made some incredibly poor choices, with lifelong implications. I have no control over anything except how I chose to respond—and how I chose to live with my choices. At the risk of sounding clichéd, I have learned a great deal. And while my losses have been significant, my gains have been extraordinary. I learned a great deal about love and true friendship, and I learned that I am stronger and more resilient than I ever imagined I could be. I learned the true meaning of hope, grief, and triumph. I also learned about pure and unadulterated fear, as well as what it means to survive. And I have learned about the human spirit and its ability to thrive against all odds.

Having been on both sides of the law, I have tried to provide a balanced, yet critical look at the process of navigating into and through our criminal justice system—as well as life and culture behind the razor wire. The heart of the book details my incarceration experience. The mistreatment of prisoners happens primarily because people (including the academics who study crime for a living) do not truly understand what it is like to be incarcerated. I have included a variety of stories and descriptions of events that feed into the devastating impact of the correctional experience. I include a brief mention of the presentence investigation process, for example. For me, it was the first real indication of society's misunderstanding about crime and contempt for those caught in the criminal justice system. I also include a section about offender "reentry" because I feel it is important to share my experiences in the job market as a convicted felon. Even with my education, I could only find work at the local roadside Farmers Market—and there only because they did not ask me to fill out a job application.

The fact that I am not the "typical" offender clearly impacts my perceptions and attitudes; it will also bias the meanings I attach to the situations and circumstances regarding my incarceration and legal experiences. At the risk of sounding condescending, I "got" the system. I was familiar with it through work and school, but I struggled tremendously. I had a certain amount of education and legal resources, and yet I was completely overwhelmed, unable to ask the right questions, unsure of the overworked and marginal legal guidance I received, and fighting the standard beliefs by both a public and a justice system that people are often "guilty upon charge." I met a significant number of women clearly lacking the resources to succeed and even survive—which should not surprise us because they typically lack even the most fundamental ability to ask for help. Most offenders lack an education level beyond junior high; they are disproportionately minority, disadvantaged, marginal members of society.

My hope is that by detailing my experiences, people will be motivated to change the system. My criticisms are harsh, but my hope is that I can stimulate a more constructive discourse; perhaps I simply need to believe that some good can come from this. Students, society, law makers, and the like need to have accurate information so that they might make better informed decisions. For many, these decisions mean life or death. One of the women who became my friend wrote the following in a letter to me shortly after my release.

> If someone you were starting to care for mentioned a mistake in their past, you would likely forgive them . . . and it wouldn't be an issue, but because it is something *you* are asking someone else to give you, well, then its something you either feel unworthy of . . . or because you've yet to fully accept and forgive yourself, you don't think you deserve it. Most of the women I've met here suffer from this. I know some wonderful women and I see the true beauty in their hearts . . . and I would not hesitate to call them friends . . . I would not hesitate to forgive them and yet they struggle to forgive themselves (as I do). (personal communication)

I have included a variety of direct quotations throughout this book. Some are from women who are currently serving time, others are from conversations I had with women while I was locked up. All of these are referenced as "personal communication." Quotations from my notes and journals are referenced as "journal entry." Following my release, my brother, as well as a number of other folks who maintained contact with me while I was incarcerated, returned all the letters I had written to them throughout my confinement, which were invaluable in chronicling my experiences.

This book is not an attempt to excuse criminal behavior or the people who violate the laws of our society and the social contract that binds us together—nor do I attempt to minimize the harm done by the crimes we have committed. Rather, it's about me and my involvement with both men and women in various parts of the criminal justice system—some working in the system, others being punished by the system. This book is about the women I met along the way and those special few with whom I spent my time on the patio. Their stories are worth telling. There is striking similarity in their narratives, as are the events and situations that have impacted their lives in tragic and unexpected ways. It is about the decisions we have made and the consequences that followed. I hope to shed light on some of the darkest and confusing corners of the world. And if I am lucky, perhaps one day I will learn to forgive myself and allow my wounds to heal.

A Personal Statement

Throughout the process of researching and writing this book, I found that I was often overcome with feelings of anxiety and frustration. There is so much information to be shared and so many details that deserve mentioning. Sifting through all that I had experienced was sometimes overwhelming and there were spans of time when I wrote nothing. The struggle for me, as both an academic and an ex-convict, was deciding how best to describe and convey my journey through the criminal justice system, my experiences preparing for and serving time in a federal correctional institute, and the painful process of picking up the pieces and trying to join a society that seemed to resent my very presence.

The difficulty was in deciding what topic(s) warranted primary attention, where to place my initial energies, and what details merited first consideration. My preliminary reaction was to focus this book on me—on the limitless depth of my embarrassment and the unbearable hold this experience has on my conscience. I feel compelled to disclose the painful experiences of my family and my friends, the losses I have felt, the indignities to which I was subjected, and my feelings of violation and the nightmares that continue today.

As I read through the notes and journal entries I maintained throughout my journey, I decided that I would first need to provide the reader with a look inside the hidden and convoluted world of government sanctioned punishment through the eyes of a woman who lived through it and all those women who will continue to live it. With that background, it would then make more sense to examine ideas about fairness, the harms of mass incarceration, the ongoing deprivation of rights, and the lack of legitimate opportunities for those who have served their time and paid their "debt" to society.

As I think back on my first days in prison, I wonder how to put into words such an extraordinary experience. I fear that those in positions of authority will deny my characterizations and that many voices in society will say "so what?" To many people, the convicted are trash. We criminals are somehow less human and less worthy. Few will show us empathy; fewer still will offer to help. Discussing the pains of imprisonment against the backdrop of an apathetic government, an unconcerned and ever-expanding system, and a judgmental public makes this task that much more important.

As a nonviolent, first-time offender, I was originally sentenced to a "work camp." Unfortunately, this facility was damaged in a hurricane, and I was subsequently assigned to a federal correctional institution. Despite my knowledge of the various processes and procedures, I was completely unprepared for what I experienced. The current treatment of those in prison reflects the views of society as a whole. The violence that takes place, the dismal medical and psychological care, the blatant abuse by staff and guards, the entirety of the efforts to break spirits and tear down the individual are tolerated and accepted. The very fact that we as convicts become accustomed to and even expect such practices and daily routines further reinforces the emotional and physical damage that occurs with even limited incarceration. The physical wounds heal, but the emotional scars will last a lifetime.

Chapter One

Women and Crime

*The soul of a man exists in the contemplation of the
nature of a woman behind bars.*
                            —Henry David Thoreau

This country's prison experiment has had ravaging effects—not
just on the offenders but also on entire groups of people and
whole communities. Many states now spend more tax money on
prisons than on university systems. As we spend more on prisons,
we have fewer dollars to devote to crucial social issues including
education, employment, health, and various economic and community problems that generate the populations that fill prisons.

The costs of our incarceration binge are not merely financial. Criminologist Todd Clear (2007) emphasizes the far-reach-
ing social impact of our extraordinary rate of incarceration.
Society must realize that it is not just the offenders who are
being punished for their illegal behaviors—children, other family members, friends and associates, and indeed entire neighborhoods are also punished. Large numbers of children are growing
up without parents; grandparents are often raising grandchil-
dren; and large portions of communities are without substantial
numbers of men. This is particularly distressing given that
many of the people in these families and communities are
minorities and marginalized members of society.

THE INCARCERATION OF WOMEN

Women are the fastest-growing segment of the criminal
justice population (Sawyer, 2018). Between 1980 and 2017, the

1

number of women in U.S. prisons has increased by more than
750%—from 26,378 to 225,060, a growth rate twice that of
men (The Sentencing Project, 2019). In 2017, 1.3 million
women were under the correctional supervision of the criminal
justice system: 9% were imprisoned, 9% were jailed, 9% were on
parole, and 70% were on probation. The imprisonment rate for
black women was 92 per 100,000; the rate for Hispanic women
was 66; and the rate for white women was 49. One-quarter of
the women in state prison were convicted of a drug offense
compared to 14% of men in state prison.

When women enter jail or prison, they do so with all the
problems that led them to the criminal activity in the first
place: poverty, addiction, histories of physical and/or sexual
abuse, family fragmentation, and the like. Economic struggles
have significant impacts on women. A staggering 60% of
women in jail have not been convicted for a crime; they are
there awaiting trial (Kajstura, 2018). Avoiding pretrial incarceration is uniquely challenging for women, particularly since the
majority of them are primary caregivers for their children.

Women in jail are even more financially challenged than
those in prison. They are held because they are unable to make
bail. They are unemployed, lack stable housing, and have mental health and/or substance abuse issues—factors that make
them more likely to be viewed as flight risks and therefore inel-
igible for bail. Incarcerated women, who have lower incomes
than incarcerated men, have an even harder time affording cash
bail. Women who could not make bail had an annual median
income of $11,071 (Rabuy & Kopf, 2016). Black women had a
median annual income of only $9,083. Even if bail is granted,
many women do not have the funds to post. As a result,
women spend far more time in jail awaiting trial.

The increase in women involved in the justice system can
be traced to changes in state and national drug policies that
mandated prison terms for even relatively low-level drug
offenses, changes in law enforcement practices (particularly
those targeting minority neighborhoods), and post-conviction
barriers to reentry (The Sentencing Project, 2019). Once
released, women find themselves restricted from governmental
assistance programs such as housing, employment, education,
and subsistence benefits. By statute, many states ban people
convicted of specific crimes from working in industries such as

nursing, childcare, and home health care—three fields in which many poor women and women of color are disproportionately concentrated. These barriers make recidivism more likely.

Increasing arrests for property and public order offenses are partly responsible for increased numbers of incarcerated women (Shelden & Vasiliev, 2018). However, the most influential factor in this nation's exploding prison population has been the "war on drugs." This war has had particularly devastating effects on women. Women are now more likely than men to serve time for drug offenses and are subjected to increasingly punitive law enforcement and sentencing practices. The increase in the proportion of women sentenced for property crime reflects their greater economic disadvantage prior to incarceration. Prison has become a first response for female criminality. Looking more closely at the personal and structural influences in their lives reveals ruinous pathways to crime, and the devastating effects of relying solely on punishment and retribution to address crime.

The one-size-fits-all incarceration policies currently in place often mask the fact that many women are particularly (and disproportionately) vulnerable to a host of risk factors that increase the likelihood of becoming involved in the criminal justice system. The vast majority of women in prison (85–90%) have a history of being victims of violence prior to their incarceration, including domestic violence, rape, sexual assault, and child abuse. Racial disparities are particularly significant as girls of color who are victims of abuse are more likely to be processed by the criminal justice system and labeled as offenders than are white girls, who have a better chance of being treated as victims and referred to child welfare and mental health systems. In addition to intimate partner violence, other risk factors contributing to women's criminal behavior include substance abuse and mental illness. It is estimated that up to 80% of women prisoners suffer from substance addiction (Smith, 2017). Research indicates that it would be much more *cost effective* to treat these women than to imprison them—and costs to society extend far beyond the financial costs of a stay in jail or prison.

SOCIETAL COSTS OF MASS INCARCERATION

The growth of the female prison population has a unique and particularly devastating effect on families and communities. Sexual violence, substance abuse, and poverty are all strongly correlated with women's incarceration (Owen, Wells, & Pollock, 2017). Unfortunately, rather than provide "front-end" care (medical, prenatal education, childcare, etc) that could help disadvantaged women live healthy, secure, productive lives, we blindly punish criminal behavior at significant personal and social expense. "For women whose pathways lead them to prison such disadvantages are replicated and often magnified inside prison, which, in turn, increases the threats to their already tenuous sense of safety and well-being" (p. 2).

Women of color experience all of these factors at disproportionate rates, which translate to a greater likelihood of becoming entangled in the criminal justice system. Of women state and federal prisoners between the ages of 18 and 24, 7% were white compared to 11% each of black and Hispanic prisoners (Bronson & Carson, 2019). Prisons fail in providing care and custody of prisoners; instead, they sustain unsafe conditions. Existing prison conditions, such as inadequate housing, untreated disease, minimal medical care, and inferior nutrition, create a context of risk and threat to women's well-being. Aspects of operational practice, such as gender-neutral classification systems and lack of women-centered services, also undermine women's ability to live safely inside prison (Owens et al., 2017).

Much of the public is unaware of the cyclical and generational nature of crime, abuse, violence and poverty. Imprisoning women as accelerated rates has resulted in a significant number of children who suffer from their mother's incarceration and the loss of family ties (Bandele, 2017). Eighty percent of women in jails are mothers, most of whom were the primary caretakers of their children (Kajstura, 2018). More than 5 million children have had a parent incarcerated at some point in their lives (The Annie E. Casey Foundation, 2016). The likelihood that children will have parents who are incarcerated is disproportionately linked to race. African American children are 7 times more likely to have a parent incarcerated compared to white children, and Hispanic children are 2 times more likely. "Having a parent incarcerated is a stressful, traumatic experience of the same magnitude as abuse, domestic violence and divorce, and with potentially lasting negative impact on a child's well-being" (p. 3). Children of incarcerated parents are more likely to drop out of school, engage in delinquency, and subsequently be incarcerated themselves (Arditti, 2012).

> I got to call the woman who has my daughter. I had not spoken to her in four years. I hate being so far away from her and my momma. Guess what? She spoke to me . . . my daughter spoke to me. I have only seen her four times since I gave birth to her in prison when I first got locked up. . . . Can you believe it? She talked to me. (personal communication)

The intersection of poverty, race, and gender increase the vulnerability of women to crime and imprisonment (Owens et al., 2017). Prisons are the default system for managing people disadvantaged through intersectional inequalities. "Women's prisons provide a stark example of these intersecting and hierarchical forms of discrimination against women, the poor, and communities of color" (p. 4). Incarcerated women have experienced—and continue to experience—institutionalized racism, victimization, and marginalization.

FINANCIAL COSTS OF MASS INCARCERATION

In addition to the extraordinary social impact of this country's mass incarceration binge, we cannot ignore the devastating financial costs—to society as a whole and to the families and individuals directly impacted by incarceration. The imprisonment boom costs the government and families of justice-involved people at least $182 billion every year (Wagner & Rabuy, 2017). It is important to note that this figure is larger than that documented by the Bureau of Justice Statistics (BJS), which states a cost of $81 million. The key difference lies in the fact that the BJS addresses the costs of running just the corrections system (prisons, jails, parole, and probation). Only identifying the specific correctional expenses misses the costs associated with law enforcement and the court system. Such a narrow financial view also overlooks the enormous amount of money paid by the families who support their incarcerated loved ones. Privatizing services like phone calls, medical care, commissary, etc. trims the expenses for prisons and jails but displaces them onto families and hides the true cost of mass incarceration (Sawyer & Wagner, 2019).

The harm done by criminals is indeed real, but as this book will suggest, the justice system chooses to criminalize only certain people and only certain crimes. Bias against the poor starts early, particularly when legislators decide what is (and is not) considered criminal. Many of the ways in which the well-off victimize society (deadly pollution, unsafe working conditions, hazardous products, tainted food) are not even defined as crimes, although they do more harm and cost society more money than acts treated as criminal (Reiman & Leighton, 2017).

The following comments address our society's general tendency to dole out absurdly long sentences for first-time, nonviolent crimes. The practice creates a hefty price tag for society to pay (with very little return on their investment) and an oppressive personal burden for the woman and her family.

> I got caught up in selling drugs to support me and my family. It was wrong, I know that. But I was pregnant at 12 (by my dad—not that the police cared), and I dropped out of school way too soon because of it. So I sold drugs. I was 23 when I got here. I've done a dime already [10 years]. I've got life to do, and all those people who turned on me are already out. How am I going to spend my life in here? (personal communication)

> This is my first time in prison, I've done 7 years of my life sentence for conspiracy to distribute heroin. Life, mommy, can you imagine? ["Mommy" is typically a term of respect and affection for older inmates.] I've tried to kill myself twice. Prison is bad alright. It's fucked with my head. (personal communication)

It should come as no surprise that our prisons and jails predominantly confine the poor. At each step, from arrest to sentencing, the possibility of becoming involved in the justice system is far less likely as wealth increases. Having social and personal capital insulates the well-off from the consequences of crime; it does not mean they are not engaging in criminal behavior. The female prisoners I met, and the thousands more I did not, continue to be drawn from the most economically and socially disadvantaged segments of society, and these women have more extensive histories of disability and disadvantage. The prison experience furthers exacerbates their marginalization—through brutality and humiliation, but also in relation to financial debt. The struggles of women inmates are made worse through prison monopolies governing commissaries, phone calls, and for some prisons, digital exploitation (charging extraordinary fees for internet minutes and device usage).

Prison commissaries are an essential part of prison life, but they have become a financial burden for many prisoners and their families. The debt often follows an individual even after release from prison. Serving as the core of the prison retail market, commissaries represent a common way in which prisons shift the costs of confinement to incarcerated people and their families. For many, this makes sense; society should not have to bear the entire costs of an inmate's wrongdoing. What is often unseen is that many of the fees attached to incarceration enrich private companies, rather than going back into the community.

The financial exploitation of incarcerated people is evidenced by the outrageous prices charged for simple services like phone calls and email (Raher, 2018). When it comes to prison commissaries, however, the prices themselves can be problematic. It seems cruel to force the families of the incarcerated to pay for basic necessities, especially when these folks cannot afford it. In the long-term, when incarcerated people can't afford goods and services vital to their well-being, society pays the price. In the short-term, however, these costs are falling on family members who are often poor and disproportionately from communities of color. "If the cost of food and soap is too much for states to bear, they should find ways to reduce the number of people in prison, rather than nickel-and-diming incarcerated people and their families" (p. 12).

One has to wonder who it is that benefits from mass incarceration, when we know it is certainly not the offenders themselves. The arbitrary nature of the treatment prisoners receive once they are locked up, the violence that surrounds them, the lack of effective counseling or beneficial job training taking place in many correctional facilities, and the ever-increasing barriers to successful reentry all but guarantee that an offender will recidivate. The philosophy that we build prisons to prevent crime is foolish and dangerous.

Chapter Two

The Process Is the Punishment

I committed my crime in the state of Washington. In 2004 I was charged in the Eastern District of Washington with one count of "making a false statement to a federal officer." At the time of my crime, I was 38 years old and was about to complete my PhD in criminal justice, forensic psychology, and social deviance at Washington State University. I received an offer for a full-time tenure track teaching position at a regional university in Florida. After relocating, I taught for one year before federal marshals showed up on my doorstep with a warrant for my arrest. The consequences of my crime weighed heavy on my mind—not just because I was terrified of being caught but also because I knew there were other people who were negatively impacted by my decisions. Selfishly, I lived each day worried that I would lose all I had worked for and ashamed that I was not strong enough to admit what I had done. I often thought about calling the officials, but fear and embarrassment paralyzed me. Admittedly there was a strange sense of relief when the marshals showed up at my door. I was exhausted from carrying this burden alone.

> I have tried hard to own the choices I have made, and I know I've no excuses for the predicament I find myself in. While I certainly don't claim innocence, I do believe my sentence was excessive. At the very least, I believe my time could have been so much better spent (volunteering or teaching at local schools or with high-risk youth/individuals, etc.). I cannot deny feelings of self-pity, which I also often see in the women around me. Having said that, I am surprised by the number of women who've openly and actively taken responsibility for the things they've done,

9

the crimes they've committed, and the hurt they've caused others along the way. Time changes everything, and perhaps that is what happens here—time to reflect back at the various opportunities I had to change the course of my life, time to question both the good and the bad, time to embrace new challenges, and the belief that everything happens for a reason. (journal entry)

There were several months between my resignation from the university and the day I walked into prison. During this time, I worked at a small Farmers Market making minimum wage. The dramatic downshift in my income made paying bills, travel expenses, and legal fees incredibly challenging. I flew back to Washington several times over the course of my case to meet with a probation officer for my presentence investigation (PSI), various meetings with my public defender, and my sentencing. Making a false statement to a federal officer carries a sentence of 6 months to five years. My attorney sought a sentence of straight probation, but the judge sentenced me to 6 months of incarceration. Because I was living in Florida, had community ties, and friends and family in the area, I was able to petition the courts to serve my time in Florida. I was originally sentenced to 6 months at a work camp in Marianna, Florida. When that facility was damaged in a hurricane, I was subsequently assigned to the Federal Correctional Institute in Tallahassee, Florida. I served my time and was released in May 2005. Following my release, I spent 5 years on supervised probation.

I hate that he shows up here in full tactical SWAT gear, how many fucking guns, knives, and cans of pepper spray does he really need? Jackass. I live in a nice albeit empty apartment with 2 cats—I'm such a threat! The criminologist in me knows he needs to be prepared for any uncertain event, that he probably does deal with volatile and unpredictable situations and people, and that he needs to do what he can to protect himself, I get that. It's just me—a sad reflection of how I feel about myself. I hate how insignificant I feel when he stares at me, judging and questioning. I hope I can teach my students compassion. . . . I guess I also have to be willing to show him compassion for the job he has to do. I'm not sure I'm ready for that yet. (journal entry related to house checks by my probation officer after I was released)

THE JUDGMENT BEGINS

A presentence investigation (PSI) is performed at the investigative stages of a case. The supervising probation officer gathers important details about the offender: background information, lists of work and leisure activities, and information from conversations with friends, family, and coworkers. The report contains specific information about one's education, previous employment, and family. It also outlines any prior criminal record, describes interviews with neighbors or associates, and includes a section on mental and physical conditions the offender might have. The PSI serves as the basis for sentencing and influences whether the convicted defendant will be granted community release or sentenced to secure confinement (Shelden, Brown, Miller, & Fritzler, 2016). At the conclusion of most presentence investigations, a recommendation is made to the presiding judge that reflects the department's sentencing posture on the case. This is a crucial aspect of the report; frequently the sentencing judge follows the probation department's recommendation. This proved *not* to be the case for me. The probation officer requested a community sentence of probation, but the judge believed a sentence of incarceration was more fitting.

Having a complete stranger "evaluate" my life was intrusive and unsettling; I found myself incredibly defensive about even the most minute detail. The PSI made me painfully aware of the gravity of my situation and demonstrated the contempt that many "officials" have for offenders. I experienced a distant, overworked and seemingly unconcerned public defender and a judge whose disdain was palpable. The personal and moral judgment of the probation officer should not have been a surprise. I am not denying personal responsibility; I have tried very hard to make sure people know that I "own" the choices that landed me in prison.

My criticisms stem from a different perspective. It is as if one moment in time negates an entire lifetime of good (or at least marginal) behavior. In an instant, my grievous choice transformed me from good to bad, from valued to worthless, from human to trash. I am not necessarily seeking sympathy for offenders, but I am asking that we not lose sight of the fact that criminal or not, offenders are human. People working in and around the criminal justice system, as well as the public, should be aware that there is not a one-size-fits-all criminal label. Criminal behavior exists on a continuum, and all offenders are not identical. If our system is to be one that effectively *corrects* (as in the correctional system), there has to be a willingness to separate the person from the behavior, I made a bad choice, but that does not (or should not) make me a bad person. It may seem like a silly game of semantics, but to me, as well as to the women I met, this distinction carries significant importance.

> I never meant to be a piece of shit, but everything I have ever done seemed to lead me in that direction. (personal communication)

> I've never been seen. Not by my mom when she was high or my stepdad when he was screwing me. Not by the juvie system where there were so many of us or the foster family who used me as a meal ticket. I was not seen by the pimp who beat me and passed me around, the hood cops always on me, or the judge that looked right through me. They don't see me. Why would I be seen here in this cage? Who will see me in the future when I can't stand to see myself in the mirror? (personal communication)

As I read through the report written by the probation officer, I was overcome with both sadness and anger, and it took me time to truly understand why. In the process of completing the PSI, an outsider was making a biased assessment about my life, every move my family ever made, every relationship I'd ever had, the miscellany of successes and failures in my life. It was painful to see my history through the eyes of another. It was difficult to accept the various inferences and interpretations of every job or every friendship, all taken out of context—assessed by someone who knew absolutely nothing about me. This court-appointed officer is supposed to be an objective individual, but the process of assigning *value* to my life felt biased and prejudicial. It's as if everything an offender has done or experienced in his/her life up until that point can be deciphered and molded into an "explanation" of why the crime was committed. My presentence report did little to capture the reality of my crime or the reasons why I behaved as I did.

The PSI was indeed excruciating, but I was similarly tormented by the media—even secondhand. To this day, I have not read the articles written about me or my case. Friends and family read the articles or watched the news clips and relayed some of the information to me. Occasionally there would be a kernel of truth in the midst of speculation and half-truths. The torment was not just over my offense; rather, it was the overall media approach to and treatment of all people linked to crime.

Popular media condition public expectations for how the criminal justice system functions (or *ought* to function). They also provide a paradigm for how the various news stories are told to society or the broader public (Kappeler & Potter, 2018). One cannot open the newspaper or watch the evening news without being inundated with accounts of violence and crime. Very few people understand that violence and street crime represent a very small proportion of the overall crime rate. In some respects, it isn't the public's fault. How can we expect them to make rational informed decisions when they rarely have accurate information? Keeping the public fearful serves special interests: the reelection of public officials, increased budgets for the justice system and its employees, and companies that sell items for personal security (guns, security systems, etc.). Another disturbing aspect of how media frame crime is that the public believes it has the right to look into the private lives of victims and offenders. Being a criminal erases our most fundamental right to privacy; the most intimate and personal details of someone's life, even if unrelated to the crime committed, are considered fair game. People make value judgments based on distorted facts, half-truths, and story lines created to sell an agenda.

> "You should be brutally raped and beaten . . . you are a cunt! You should die!" (An email I received from a stranger)

Not only are arrestees regarded as guilty *until proven innocent* in this country, but they are also portrayed as remorseless, cunning, and sociopathic by mainstream media. The public sees criminals as one-dimensional characters, bereft of everything human. The picture painted is us versus them, good versus evil, the saintly and the diabolical. This runs counter to the women and men I met along the way who proved to me that those of us touched by the criminal justice system *do* see things differently; we are not a blank canvas of evil. We have depth and meaning and intelligence. Lamentably, our lives and our worth are rendered unworthy in mainstream media accounts. One moment in time defines people irrevocably as "criminal" "bad" "other" and "damaged."

I cannot believe it is over—at least the prison portion. I met with my new PO [probation officer] and his supervisor today. My first impression of him was ok—I don't think many government officials think about their interactions with "clients" or the impact this relationship has on our reintegration. And, given my negative experience with attorneys, the judge, the marshals, the correctional staff, I wondered why this relationship would be any different. Even with limited exposure to the cruel and unrelenting prison system, self-image and self-awareness have been shattered. I have spent the last year or so feeling broken and empty. As criminals, we already criticize ourselves, it really isn't necessary for those working with us to demean us or to humiliate us further—we get it! We know the contempt and disapproval that you feel towards us. (journal entry)

As I sat in the waiting room of the probation office with some 20 other criminals waiting for DNA tests and random urine analyses, I couldn't help but feel an odd mixture of both comfort and humiliation. (journal entry)

I did have one call with A. this week, I'm grateful my PO allows me contact with some of the women I met at FCI. As we talked it was like being back on the patio all over again. All those feelings rushed back over both of us (she was released the same day I was): where we'd been, what we'd seen and done, and how it all has impacted our lives, in general and in very specific ways. I hate that I don't sleep without medication, I hate that my body gets tense and my anxiety levels rise at 4 p.m. and 10 p.m. (times of daily counts). I'm anxious out in public, as if I wear a scarlet F for felon—how I miss the lack of judgment in prison. (journal entry)

I'm very ready to leave, I have seen enough degradation and indignities to last me a lifetime! I don't know if I'll ever really be able to put this experience into words, or to write about it in such a way as to retain the perceptions, the frustration (and the pain), and the lived experiences of the women I have met! (journal entry)

DECIDING TO LIVE

Two days have passed since my original sentence was handed down. I am still numb inside, and I continue to struggle for reasons to live. I know I am the one who made the choices that got me here in the first place, and I know I have to pay the consequences—I just never imagined I would have to pay this much. (journal entry)

As I headed back home to Florida following the sentencing in my case, I was hard-pressed to keep a coherent thought in my head. I was feeling so much at the time, and yet feeling nothing at all. As I listened to the hum of the airplane, the clouds around me created an odd sense of comfort, somehow insulating me from the chaos in the life that awaited me. My mind raced with the options I was facing. My lawyer filed a "motion to reconsider"—an effort essentially asking the judge to change his mind, a long shot by any stretch of the imagination. I also had the option of filing an appeal, a process that, like most things in the criminal justice field, moves slowly. I wanted this to be over, and the thought of dragging this out another 9 to 12 months seemed like a slow and painful death. And even if I *were* to be successful in my appeal, a period of incarceration was allowable under the guidelines. To think that I would wait—barely making ends meet with my cashier job at the local Farmers Market, delaying closure for family and friends, and knowing I might be locked up anyway—was too unbearable. I didn't think I could survive a life in limbo. I needed to be on the other side of all that had happened, and all that was going to happen. The uncertainly made me weary, and the vision of what lay ahead seemed insurmountable. There was a part of me that didn't want to go on; yet another part of me was determined to overcome this and not let it define me.

Most days I felt lost and weak, empty and hopeless, but there were those rarest of moments when I wanted to live, and I wanted to go on. Many will not understand my suicidal thoughts—believing that my sentence was not so significant as to warrant such a melodramatic outcome. Perhaps these folks are right, but in many of my most desperate moments, death seemed so much easier. I needed time and distance. I needed to be able to look back over this experience with better clarity and faith in the notion that things happen for a reason. In the days that followed, I began to see that there was a path for me to take. I began to realize that all of this could not be in vain, that some seed of good had to come from this. I am still hesitant to say that this has all been worthwhile, but a number of significant things have happened as a result of this fateful experience.

A number of people have entered my life or changed "roles" in my life, bringing me strength and a renewed sense of purpose. I have found extraordinary support from those around me and have truly been touched by people and their capacity to love and forgive. I found that I often underestimated the willingness of others to see past my illegal behavior. I have been pleasantly surprised at those around me who are able to separate the behavior from the person. Likewise, I was hurt by some people I considered friends. They made it clear that what was once considered unconditional love and friendship did indeed have boundaries. Those friendships were fractured by the perceptions that recast me as someone unworthy.

Following my original sentence, I was released on my own recognizance (ROR). This meant that I did not have to immediately report to the institution to begin serving my time. My attorney filed a "motion to stay" challenging the judge's decision and 6-month prison sentence. A stay of proceedings is a ruling by the court in both civil and criminal procedures that halts further legal processing in a case where an appeal has been filed.

I considered myself fortunate in that I would have time to get my affairs in order before going to prison. I wondered though, how one *plans* for this. I was lucky in the sense that I had time to put my financial and personal business in order; I would need to put furniture in storage, methodically outline how and when (and if) my existing bills would be paid, find a place to store my vehicle, and beg friends to watch the animals I was afraid of losing. Only later would I realize that planning to go in would be far easier than arranging to come out.

Our motion to stay request was denied. After a number of conversations with my lawyer, I ultimately decided to withdraw my appeal. The waiting and not knowing stretched over months; the uncertainty was agonizing. I felt paralyzed in that moment of time—I could not rewind time to *take back* my crime, and I could not move forward to *atone for* my crime. I finally made the decision to get on with my life and to stop waiting and hoping for a different outcome. I needed to pay my "debt" and move on. I felt powerless throughout most of my criminal justice processing, and perhaps this was one way for me to feel as if I had regained a modicum of control. I found some comfort in the knowledge that I would be serving my time in a work camp, a very minimum-security level facility for nonviolent and low-risk offenders.

Unfortunately, this sense of having a "do-able sentence" was brief. A hurricane damaged the work camp to which I was designated, and I was subsequently reassigned to FCI Tallahassee. Compared to male offenders, there are relatively few female offenders, and therefore very few female correctional facilities. Having only a small number of facilities, placement based on security levels becomes a moot point. As I would soon discover, FCI Tallahassee not only housed first-time nonviolent offenders like me, it also housed a substantial number of serious, chronic, and violent offenders.

Much of this book addresses the fragmented and confusing criminal justice process. I observed this firsthand shortly after my arrest; what I experienced could only be categorized as an ill-conceived, intentionally ineffective obstacle course. Given my post-secondary education and my years of working professionally in the field, I thought I knew the steps in offender processing, I thought I knew who to ask what, and I thought I knew what to expect—I could *not* have been more wrong. This was never more apparent than when I withdrew my appeal and asked to begin my serving my sentence. At this time, I was simultaneously answering to my attorney, my community supervision officer, the correctional officials at both the Marianna work camp and FCI Tallahassee, and the federal marshals who are typically responsible for transporting federal prisoners.

While in graduate school, I had taken several classes in organizational behavior and the administration of justice. Much of our reading for these classes centered on the concept of "bureaucracy"—a way of administratively organizing large numbers of people who are expected to work together. The main challenges of a bureaucratic agency are its inflexibility, the incessant red tape, and the incredibly slow decision making. There could not have been a better description of what ensued after requesting that I be allowed to self-surrender.

My lawyer instructed me to contact the intake officer at Marianna; the work camp personnel then referred me to the people at FCI Tallahassee; the FCI information desk referred me back to my attorney. I was unable to get a solid (reasonable) answer from any of them. I then approached my community supervisor who told me the U.S. Marshal Service would be in charge of "taking me in." The Service replied back that because I was effectively turning myself in, I could simply show up at the designated facility (which, at this point, was still the work camp). After several months of infuriating phone calls, letters, and waiting for emails that never arrived (plus the self-doubt about not following through with my appeals process), I was finally "allowed" to report to FCI Tallahassee on my specified date in November. A friend drove me to Tallahassee—we had a nice dinner, commiserated over a few beers, and tried to prepare for what the morning might bring. Playing continually in my head was my favorite song by Five Stairsteps, "O-o-h Child." I fervently hoped their lyrics about things getting easier would be true—and that when the nightmare ended, I would be walking in the rays of a beautiful sun of a much brighter world. [My brother would play the song for me over the phone several times during the course of my incarceration.]

Chapter Three

Becoming a Convict

You become. It takes a long time. That's why it doesn't often happen to people who break easily, or have sharp edges, or have to be carefully kept. Generally, by the time you are Real, most of your hair has been loved off, and your eyes drop out and you get loose in the joints and very shabby. But these things don't matter at all, because once you are Real you can't be ugly, except to people who don't understand.

—The Velveteen Rabbit

INTAKE, CLASSIFICATION, AND THE UNIT TEAM

One of the biggest differences between facilities for men and women is the absence of custody-graded institutions for women. Men are sent to a prison that most often matches the risk they present. Because women in general pose little risk (e.g., escape, assaults on inmates or officers), some argue that classification systems for women should focus on needs, including such factors as drug use, mental illness, prior victimization, special medical needs, and occupational deficiencies (Pollock, 2014).

Regardless of where you serve your time, introduction to the prison world is quite similar. Inmates are stripped of their civilian status and assimilated into the convict culture. This process of entry into prison society involves a dehumanizing sequence of shedding one's outer identity and becoming a number, with prison clothes, prison rule books, and prison toiletries. These entry procedures are extraordinarily frightening and alienating.

During the first days of a prison sentence, we're indoctrinated to the prison world. Prison rules are explained, facility and

19

unit procedures are described, and available programs are detailed. We are apprised of the various rules and regulations and are told what is expected of us. Upon entry, we are fingerprinted and photographed, stripped, searched, and given prison clothing. Depending on the facility, reception may include a medical examination, a psychiatric evaluation, and educational testing. This entire process, which for me was carried out over the course of about 2 weeks, was particularly stressful and degrading.

When I first arrived, everything was completely foreign. The hard part for me was trying to reconcile the dissonance in my head of where I'd come from and how far I had fallen. Even now, when I close my eyes, I can still see, and smell, and hear the inside of the prison. Some days it feels so heavy and tangible. As a first-time inmate, I found myself in an extremely confusing and chaotic world where nothing seemed to make sense and time seemed to stand still. The constant struggle to take in everything and everyone around me left me sick and exhausted. There were so many rules and expectations. Some were written; most were not. It doesn't take an inmate long to realize there are FBOP (Federal Bureau of Prisons) guidelines, and then there are convict guidelines—strict adherence to both is necessary. The reality of my newfound criminal status and the constant reminders of my failed life filled me with dread. The lack of hope I felt when I thought about what life would hold for me upon release consumed me. I was one of "them" now. Only recently have I fully understood how deeply I was changed. Fragments of my time at FCI, and glimpses of people I met along the way, still find their way into my dreams.

I'll never forget the day I walked into prison; I have replayed that day over and over again in my head. It is difficult to know what part of the day stood out the most for me. As the receiving room cell door slammed shut for the first time, I was besieged by the gripping realization of where I was and what was to come. An eerie chill washed over me, and I felt as if I were going to pass out. At that moment, past memories and particularly those of the legal events of the most recent years engulfed me, and my head felt like it would explode. There was a gnawing fear consuming me. I remembered every prison movie I ever watched, every sensationalized media account I ever read, and all of the horror stories I ever heard, I was petrified! My emotions were all over the place; I felt everything and nothing. I fought to control the tears welling up inside me.

I felt fear in places that I didn't know existed. Empty and cold and hollow. I wish I was dead. Feeling nothing has got to be better than not knowing the pain I'm bound to encounter here. Clearly our retributive society and its prisons have figured out how to terrorize us and to instill horror in us, because what they're doing definitely works. How about karma? I used to be the person to advocate for harsh treatment of criminals, and now I'm subject to that meanness. (journal entry)

The abusive nature of the prison experience can have a devastating impact on an inmate. Upon arriving in a correctional facility, female prisoners are usually strip-searched, a process that includes a cavity search (bending over and exposing vaginal and rectal areas)—and a squat-and-cough search for contraband. In 2019, the Seventh U.S. Circuit Court of Appeals in Chicago ruled against 200 women inmates who had sued after an incident at Lincoln Correctional Center (Editorial, 2019). About 200 inmates were handcuffed, sent to a gym, ordered to take off their clothes, remove any tampons, and submit to a cavity search. The activities were visible not only to the attending guards but also to other prison staffers. By a 2–1 vote, the court ruled that prisoners have few privacy rights under existing U.S. Supreme Court precedents and that none were violated by the Lincoln guards. The courts have generally deferred to prison administrators when engaging in practices designed to preserve order and institutional security. Complicating the issue was that the Lincoln procedure was a formal training exercise to teach cadet guards how to conduct cavity searches. The judge who voted against the ruling stated that the training was not necessary since most cadets graduated without it. In addition, if the strip searches were justified, why were they conducted where people not involved in the exercise could view the "training"? "As a matter of decency, the intrusion on physical privacy should be limited to what is required for a valid purpose" (p. 13).

Many prisons, FCI Tallahassee included, conduct mandatory strip searches and/or pat-downs before and after visits with friends and family. These humiliating procedures took place in what the inmates referred to as "the shakedown shack." This degrading introduction into the prison world foreshadowed what was to come. Most toilets, showers, and cubicles offer only minimal privacy. Officers directly, or indirectly though surveillance cameras, observe inmates' bodies. For a society that shows a clear lack of empathy or support for offenders, lack of privacy in bathrooms or dressing areas probably doesn't register as violation or sexual intrusion. It is, however, a continual traumatic experience.

> This place in general, does not care about who you are or what you're capable of. They care about hiding you away so that most of society is comforted that a "criminal" is not "at large." (journal entry)

Victor Hassine (2011) described his initial classification ordeal, "I hesitated, reluctant to surrender my clothes, my last ties to freedom" (p. 18). My first strip search is forever etched in my brain. For me, it was less about my loss of freedom and individuality (at least initially), and more its demeaning and demoralizing nature. On its face, the strip search makes sense; inmates must be prevented from bringing contraband inside a facility. But I have often wondered why it was necessary that these procedures in the name of safety had to be degrading and sometimes abusive. Many women consciously weighed whether seeing friends and family for visitations was worth the search procedures that followed.

> The shakedown shack? Hell, that ain't worth no fuckin' visit from no one . . . looking in my ass and making me take my tampon in and out . . . that's bullshit, you know they only doin' that for kicks because they can. (personal communication)

A young woman was processed with me the morning I self-surrendered. It was probably one of the best things that could have happened to me as I began my carceral experience. She would become the woman I spent the most time with and with whom I still maintain a very important and enduring friendship. As I sat in the cold stark holding cell waiting to be taken to the Assessment and Orientation Unit (A & O), I watched her go through the very same "receiving" process that I had just endured. Her pale tear-stained face broke my heart, and I wondered what sort of crime she could have committed. I could see the fear and devastation on her face, and I was certain I had the same lost expression and frightened demeanor. She was pretty and young, with a wide-eyed look of bewilderment and naïveté that was a dangerous combination for a newcomer cast into the perdition of imprisonment.

It would be several days before we spoke to each other. Neither one of us spent much time off our bunks or out of our unit. One afternoon we decided to go to the dining hall together. We hoped the companionship would make the experience less frightening and potentially less dangerous.

> A. and I went to the dining hall for the first time today—
> I'm not so sure what we felt was necessarily fear, but rather
> a sense of devastation and anxiousness. Neither one of us
> felt like we belonged here, and yet we did. (journal entry)

Like me, this was her first time in prison. The amalgamation of warnings from friends and family, prurient images from television and media accounts, and stories from the convicts themselves left us unbelievably paranoid. Prior to that, the only way either one of us left the orientation unit that week was when directly told to do so by the guards on duty. Remaining isolated on our respective bunks somehow made us feel less vulnerable and better able to monitor our surroundings. It was clear we were experiencing many of the same feelings. Sharing the process of being socialized into prison culture and acquiring the convict identity that would follow us for life eased the torment.

> I hate this place. There is an awkward, nauseating aroma—
> a mixture of flowers and feminine hair products, watered-
> down disinfectant, and rotten meat (contraband left in
> someone's locker). I hate how the women smell. I hate how
> the guards smell. I hate how I smell. I hate that you can pre-
> dict how the day/evening will go by the sickening cologne
> that wafts in from the main office of the unit—the predict-
> ability of knowing which guards are on duty, whether I will
> sleep tonight, or whether it will be another night of "any-
> thing goes." I hate how the male guards leer and the female
> guards chastise. I hate this place. (journal entry)

Time has changed how I perceive and interpret my experiences at FCI Tallahassee. Although it's been over 15 years since my release, the memories remain clear and vivid. There are times I am struck by a particular smell, or a sound, or even a random face in a crowd. I am often able to tuck these thoughts away in a mental and emotional compartment that allows me to function in my day-to-day life. It does not take me long, however, to reopen and expose that place in my head, revealing the pain and the loss of self that was all around me. As convicts, we will forever be stained by the various and often blatant acts of brutality, as well as even the most subtle acts of degradation or violation and coercion couched conveniently in policy for safety and facility security.

> There's no way to know just how much prison is changing me. In my gut I always feel this huge, heavy, odd knot that presses on my insides. I ache—no doubt a medley of regret, fear, anger, and triumph (I can't believe I just wrote triumph, but *fuck you* Tallahassee, I'm surviving). The guards and the women don't deserve my fear, it's wasted on them. My dread and misery make me defiant, and I'm stronger for it. I don't want to be bitter from this; I don't want to waste whatever life I might have left focused on revenge and being angry. I hope I will be as strong when I get out. (journal entry)

> I've wondered many times why it appears that degradation is part of the treatment. If you wish these women to become "improved" by this process, then you must treat them with some level of respect, even if they don't deserve it. I have never known of any living thing that responded well to humiliation and intimidation. Why would the prison expect women to leave here better than when they arrived? Oh, they might get their GED and they might have developed some new skills through the call center (UNICOR), but if they have no pride in themselves and feel as if their mistakes were a badge everyone could see, then you've doomed them to a life they never deserved, regardless of the bad choices they made before they got here. (personal communication)

Even with short-term incarceration, I could not help but witness (and ultimately bear) the inescapable transformation of the woman I once was into the convict I became. There are many certainties in prison, not the least of which is the inevitable assimilation into a culture that is unique to convicts.

> I lied to the shrink throughout my psych eval, I would imagine most do. He stared across his desk at me with the all-too-familiar condescending gaze that I had seen a lot in the last year, so smug and so sure that I was nothing like him. Truth-be-told, I *did* fit his female convict profile, but I'll be damned if I was going to tell him that. Maybe he knew, maybe he didn't; I didn't care. I was a cliché to him. (journal entry)

HOME ON THE RANGE

Life in women's prisons both resembles and differs from that in institutions for men. Women's facilities tend to be smaller in size, with looser security and less-structured inmate-staff relationships. The underground economy is not as well developed. Overall, female prisoners seem less committed to the inmate code. Women generally serve shorter sentences then do men, so women's prison society is more fluid as new members join and others leave (Clear, Reisig, & Cole, 2019). It is important to note shifts in the female prison subculture. There is support for the idea that prisons for women are less violent, involve less gang activity, and don't have the racial tensions found in men's prisons; however, some studies indicate that the interpersonal relationships that do exist in female facilities may be less stable and less familial than in the past.

New inmates spend several weeks in G Unit for orientation. Much to my discomfort, this was also the place that held women coming back from the Special Housing Unit (SHU), also known as "the hole." These women have typically faced severe disciplinary action. Following segregation, they are "reoriented" through A & O until a bed opens up in another unit. New inmates received a copy of the "Inmate Information Handbook" and were instructed to read it completely. The handbook stated that the material included was designed to help new inmates understand what they would encounter and to assist them in their initial adjustment to institutional life. The handbook contained a section detailing the inmate's rights and responsibilities, plus a range of topics from rules and regulations, to food storage, and to items inmates were allowed to possess.

> When I first entered the compound, walking through the yard with my fish kit (a box containing an inmate's new prison-issued belongings), I saw the faces of all the women who had made this prison their home. They just stared at me. In my mind I just kept saying "oh hell no, this can't be my life! There's no way I can spend 30 months of my life here." Now one year later I see things a bit differently. I'm not ready to say that I'm a better person, but I'm getting there. (personal communication)

After being briefed about the programs and services available, we attended lectures from various staff regarding their programs and departments. A case manager was designated for each of us, and we received a medical screening by the mental health staff. At the conclusion of our A & O orientation, we were assigned a job and a unit team. A "unit" is a self-contained inmate living area that includes both housing sections and office space for unit staff. Each unit is staffed by a team of people directly responsible for the women living in a specific unit. The unit staff includes the unit manager, case manager(s), unit counselor(s), and a unit secretary. When available, although it seemed to happen very rarely, the staff psychologist, education advisor, and unit officer would sit in and take part in unit team meetings. Generally, the resolution of issues or matters of interest within the facility are addressed through this unit team. Unit teams assist in a variety of areas, such as release planning, personal and family problems, and counseling.

G unit was very much like a dorm setting: 3 floors (stories); 2 "ranges" on each floor. A range consisted of a row of cubicles (10 or 12), each holding two women. Each cubicle also displayed two small lockers that were to house any personal belongings a prisoner might have. There seemed to be a great deal of overcrowding as they also had bunk beds in the hallways (and in other units there were bunks in bathrooms and gymnasiums). Unfortunately, new friend "A" was stuck on one of those hallway cots. Privacy in prison is virtually nonexistent. Being placed out in the open not only guaranteed *even less* privacy, but it also increased one's vulnerability. It was cramped and uncomfortable—a merciless environment.

There were no "cells" in the truest sense. Rather, there were small 3-walled rooms with a fourth side open. There were no doors. Women were more or less able to come and go in each other's spaces unsupervised—and believe me, they did! The hallways were loud. The voices of both men and women echoed and reverberated throughout the building. Climbing the stairs from floor to floor was like working your way through a human obstacle course, but there was some comfort in the fact that things seemed to get quieter with each floor. We felt lucky, my new friend and I, as we were ultimately handed off to a guard monitoring the third floor. The pandemonium, the never-ending clamor, and the continuous arguing and fighting would become a routine part of our daily lives.

For the first few hours, my bunkie (one with whom you share your bunk bed) was a stunning Native American lesbian serving the 10th year of her 12-year sentence. As she hung her head over the top bunk looking down at me with a youthful and sympathetic smile, I began to cry. All of my feelings from the day burst from me almost uncontrollably at that moment. She got up and left the cube, returning a short time later with a hot cup of coffee. As she returned, she looked back over her shoulder at someone I could not see and casually exclaimed, "You're an asshole, back off." As it turned out, she was speaking to the officer in charge of our floor. She waved him off, sat down next to me, and said, "Welcome to prison." She was very eager to tell me her "story"—both personal and criminal. She was friendly and helpful, but I was also wary of what being "helpful" could mean in a prison setting. I was taken aback by how young she appeared, and I was later told she came in at the age of 19. We talked for quite some time that day. By early evening, I was moved to another cubicle where I would stay until my transition into the general population.

It was a week before I allowed myself to venture out of the observation unit. My bunkie at that time was an older Spanish woman who helped me make up my bunk that first evening (there is a very *specific* way beds were to be made to pass "inspection"). She regularly encouraged me to get out of bed and go outside. It was obvious that my behavior was typical of newcomers unfamiliar with the routine and reality of prison life. I cried all the time that first week; by week two, I only cried at night.

I quickly learned that strength and power came in a variety of ways. Self-confidence (whether it was real or faked) was a must—weakness was unacceptable. It took me awhile to understand so much of what I saw. And to this day, my interpretation of the things I witnessed and experienced continues to change.

> Time moves painfully slow around here. Time is measured by monotony and boredom. At night, time seems to stand still. I continue to wake up often throughout the night, either because I am cold, having a bad dream, or simply struck with the reality of where I am. (journal entry)

Prison life is an odd concoction of uncertainty and isolation, wrapped in monotony and predictability. Yes, we had stated rules and regulations to follow, but the inconsistencies from officer to officer, shift to shift, and day to day established a foundation where one truly didn't know what would happen from moment to moment. I'm reminded of the literature on domestic violence, where the inconsistent responses by a batterer leave a victim in a continuous hypersensitive state of walking on eggshells, unsure of what behavior will garner what response. I felt this way often while I was locked up.

I was acutely aware of my isolation, despite the fact that I was surrounded by 1,400 other women. Imprisonment purposely entails a great deal of deprivation, particularly with regards to the separation from family and friends. I remember feeling complete emptiness and awful, nagging pangs of desperation at the lack of tangible emotional support. The noise, chaos, violence, and unabashed lack of regard or concern for others contributed to my destitution.

The first weeks were by far the most painful. After that, nothing really compared to the fear and the loneliness I felt being shut away with no resources or contact with the outside world. The money I brought with me did not register into my commissary account for about three weeks. Having no access to money meant no hygiene supplies (other than those few that were prison issued), no phone calls, and no pens or pencils or paper for letters home. I had made my *one* phone call shortly after leaving the reception and receiving department; I called my brother to let him know I was checked in and officially classified. I remember thinking that I could die in here, and no one on the outside would know. That thought kept me awake many nights.

Along with our standard issue prison clothes, we were given a few personal sundries, a toothbrush, deodorant, and the like. I remember how excited I was the day I realized I had money and was now able to "shop" (in the commissary)— despite the overpriced and outdated products, I was positively overjoyed! It sounds so cliché to say how much I missed and began to treasure the little things in life, but I soon realized the devastating loss of the most fundamental and simplest of belongings would strike me many more times throughout my stay in prison. One of the strange positives that would ultimately come from this experience is the gratitude I have for many things I used to take for granted. With nothing but time on my hands, stripped of all personal and material identity, it was easy to be reflective about my life—but it also made thoughts of the future that much more daunting.

> Thoughts of my future consume me. What does my future hold? Will I be able to find a job other than the Farmer's Market? Will I ever teach again? Will I ever be credible as a professional, an academic, or as a person in general? How will I make a living? Will I be able to accept that sometimes the answer is "no"? I try to be positive and count my blessings; I want to believe and to be hopeful. I am just afraid of false expectations; I am afraid of my disappointments and letdowns; I am afraid of the uncertainty. (journal entry)

Before my money was registered into my account, one of the women was nice enough to give me a pencil, so I began my note taking, journaling, and letter writing on various scraps of paper I picked up along the way. At times I would use the back of pages torn from my FCI handbook. Other times I would use napkins or paper towels from the dining hall. My brother lovingly chided me about his efforts to decipher the information on the unconventional material used for letters. It became a game of sorts for him to discern where (and from what source) I'd obtained my writing paper. He would often say that the letters I wrote told one story, and the paper source revealed another.

> It took us a while to figure out your last letter was written on your telephone request form. I'm guessing this is where you had to list out who you want to have contact with, yes? The odd shade-the-bubbles-in part looked like those old scan forms we used to have to take school tests with. You remember those? (letter from my brother)

> Ok, you have to help us with this one . . . we've only got partial paper information. At the top it says "DOJ, UNICOR and FPI"—what the heck does that all mean? Are you sure you're not just making this stuff up to get us to spend time with our prison-based paper scavenger hunt? Is this because you're bored? Ha Ha. (letter from my brother)

My journaling was initially about getting out of prison and sorting through my feelings of the day (or night) before evolving into attempts to process all that was going on around me. Many convict criminologists (a nationally recognized group that emerged as a result of the frustrations experienced by ex-convict academics over the misrepresentations of scholars, the media and government about crime and corrections) kept in touch with me throughout my journey into and out of prison. They suggested I keep a personal diary not only as a way to deal with my fear and anxiety—but also as a way to chronicle my day-to-day experiences to shed light on the reality of living in a women's prison. I am grateful for their advice; much of this book comes from those diary notes, daily logs, and the letters I had written and received from friends and family.

> The hardest part for me is waiting to hear my name at mail call and never hearing it. (personal communication)

My first trip to the commissary made it possible for me to take a shower and actually enjoy it (relatively speaking, of course). It was amazing how just a few simple hygiene products could make such a tremendous difference. I was equally pleased to learn that there were indeed individual showers, although I was told this was indicative *only* of the A & O Unit, so I had better enjoy it while I could. Much to my dismay, the toilets were not so private. Each cubicle did have its own, complete with a little shower curtain-type cover. However, I was mortified when I realized that, when seated, your ass was right next to the bunk (*and head*) of the woman on the bottom bunk. Both friends and family will tell you that I have always been a fairly modest person, but it didn't take long to realize there was no room for private or reticent behavior in prison. I will return to the topic of the commissary later in the book.

> I purchased a pair of sweats, a thermal shirt, and a pair of socks—there was an explosion in the laundry room on Wednesday, so blankets and socks are difficult to come by! My most coveted purchases of the night, however, were a mug, instant coffee, and chapstick (my lips have been so chapped, I've been using butter "kiped" from the dining hall)—how cliché am I if I say prison is about losing the simple things in life? I stood in line for nearly 3 hours, but it was *so* worth it! (letter to my brother)

THE COMPOUND

The overall facility was larger than I had expected, with a number of administrative buildings, housing units, and a variety of other buildings I would slowly learn about. All of this was surrounded by rows and rows of razor wire, never once letting us forget where we were. In addition to the housing units, the compound also included a medical building that was attached to the administration building, which also housed the lieutenant's office. These higher-ranking guards were feared by most of us, and we all knew no good would come from being summoned up to that office (a painful experience I endured only once). There is a large education building with a variety of classrooms, a computer programming annex, the library, and several reading areas.

Directly across from G unit was the dining hall. There was a fairly large recreation center on the second floor where women could go to play board games, exercise, or work on arts and craft projects. There was also a stage in this room where periodic plays and concerts took place. Attached to the dining hall was the chapel building, with a number of library-type rooms, singing rooms, and a large, lovely sanctuary. Outside the wires and just down the hill, was a detention center that housed administrative security-level male inmates (the men's Federal Department of Corrections). The whole place is quite large and ominous on the outside, but far more appealing (I *guess*) on the inside.

> I was given a list of things that can be bought at the "store" and I am amazed—the gals in here are making all kinds of things for dinner. I am excited because I will actually be able to get things like coffee and tweezers (it really *is* the little things in life). Oddly enough, we can't have tape, but we can have tweezers and scissors—go figure! (journal entry)

> We do have a TV on this range, but unfortunately, it appears to be permanently on the Spanish television channel—I realized I should have paid better attention to my college Spanish courses! (letter to brother)

I liked being in the G unit; unfortunately, women are typically transferred after several weeks. With the exception of a few isolated incidents, the overall feel of the observation unit was fairly peaceful and relaxed (within the prison context). I was surprised at how nice the women were around me, but I think it helped that I more or less aligned myself with some of the older women, being ever so cautious of course! Aside from the troublemakers, the gang bangers, and the "crack whores" (as defined by the women themselves), many of the women appeared content doing their time with as little conflict and/or distraction as possible. I was assigned to B unit once I finished my time in the observation unit—according to the ladies, that would be a good thing! It would be at least 2 weeks before I got a job. Until then, I would have to go through programs and classes that were supposed to "orientate" me to the system.

Much of my early time was spent seeking out my case manager/counselor or sitting for hours on end at the medical clinic waiting to complete my physical. The women joked, often in frustration, that everything in prison was "hurry up and wait." Perhaps it wasn't intentional, but it sure felt to us as if we were simply not worth the time of those we sought to see. As is the case in many correctional facilities across the country, FCI Tallahassee was overcrowded and understaffed. It was ominous, and terrifying, and it reeked of hopelessness. I desperately wanted out of here!

Getting "cleared" medically meant that an inmate could finally begin working. All of the inmates were expected to maintain a regular job assignment. The majority job assignments were controlled through a system that provided automatic monetary payment for work. This meant that our money was directly deposited—minus any court fees, restitution, or other types of administrative fines an inmate had to pay. Much of my education center pay was withheld and paid towards the balance of court fees I still had pending. The financial burden that followed me into prison was related to administrative and processing fees, rather than charges pertaining to my actual stay in prison.

The justice system is replete with multiple opportunities for offenders to be charged fees in an attempt to shift costs from the government to the offender. However, unlike fines that are designed to punish the offender and/or pay back victims, "user fees" are intended to raise revenue and supplement state and local budgets. National media (particularly after the death of Michael Brown in Ferguson, Missouri) have reported the overreliance on court fees as a primary source of revenue for many jurisdictions—a burden that too frequently falls on overpoliced minority districts.

Courts impose monetary sanctions on convicted individuals, as discussed in the section on the financial costs of mass incarceration, fees are attached to every aspect of the criminal justice system. Those fees must be paid—either by the offender or by his/her family (or both). An estimated 10 million people owe more than $50 billion in debt resulting from their involvement in the criminal justice system (Evans, 2014). Most states have devised ways to take money from a prisoner's commissary account to pay for the costs of housing them. Fees associated with the pay-to-stay movement include medical expenses (Eisen, 2015). Some states charge offenders for clothing (Louisiana), while other states (Missouri) charge offenders for transportation, room, board, security, and other living expenses.

> Individuals are leaving jails and prisons with a mountain of debt, much of it stemming from the fees they incurred behind bars, where a short telephone call home can cost as much as $20. These former inmates can face aggressive collection tactics, including additional fines, driver's license suspension, or, in some cases, reincarceration. (p. 2)

It is worth noting that there are a number of small city jails that, for a fee, allow wealthier offenders to "upgrade" their jail conditions to a newer and more private "cell." Interestingly, the type of crime for which one is convicted bears no relation to the ability of an inmate to obtain one of these modernized cells, as many of these offenders are serving time because of serious and violent crimes. Building new facilities was meant to be the answer to jail overcrowding, but it has now morphed into yet another example of our two-tiered system of justice (one for the wealthy and one for the poor).

Federal Prison Industries (FPI), for those inmates working for UNICOR, utilized a separate pay scale. UNICOR factories use inmate labor to provide a variety of products and services, from making prison uniforms to data entry processing. At FCI Tallahassee, selected inmates worked in contact centers focused on voice-based services including 411 information call centers. Working for FPI was preferable because the pay was substantially better—some women in UNICOR made over a dollar an hour, which is of course far better than the 11 to 20 cents an hour for other jobs across the prison. Many jobs in prison are mundane and require very little intellectual stimulation—but having any job was typically preferable to the idle time spent doing nothing. However, overcrowding in many facilities has made it difficult to provide jobs for everyone.

The library was small, but bright and oddly comfortable. It resembled a modest medical office waiting room. I didn't know at the time, but this space would become a salvation amidst a world of chaos and confusion. Most of the books were old and outdated, but the library did provide books from a number of different genres, and across a litany of topics. I had spent the last five or six years in graduate school reading the books assigned to me. For the first time in years, I was now able to read for fun. (Ok, maybe not *for fun*, but at least I now had the opportunity to read books I might not otherwise have taken the time to read.)

Within the education center (which includes a number of classrooms, offices, and the law library) there was a small but accommodating area for reading magazines. Several months into my sentence, it became one of my favorite places to sit alone or with friends. We would get together to share our likes and dislikes while we looked through travel, cooking, home, and garden magazines. We would discuss recipes, regional traditional dishes, and the favorite meals we liked to cook. The vacation magazines were a double-edged sword—both joyous and cruel. Pictures of white sandy beaches where we longed to lie in the sun, warm and cozy log cabins adorned with fireplaces and surrounded by majestic mountains, and a menagerie of other travel hot spots tantalized and teased us. They provided a much-needed emotional escape to a world that seemed magical and cathartic; yet they were also devastatingly painful, subtly reminding us of the lives few would ever have.

During the weekday we had to get up at 6 a.m. and have our cubbies made and organized by 7:30 a.m. Each morning our "cubes" had to be swept, mopped, cleaned, and ready for inspection. We were expected to eat, be dressed, and be at our jobs (or school) by the 7:30 a.m. "call-out." If you did not work in the morning or chose not to go to breakfast, you still had to have your bunk made and cube ready; you were only allowed to be on top of your bunk. On the weekends and holidays, we were allowed to sleep until 10 a.m., although bunks and cubes still needed to be inspection-ready at the later time. I was initially very excited about the prospect of sleeping in; however, I soon realized it would be nearly impossible to do so.

We had two "counts" daily, 4 p.m. and 10 p.m. On certain occasions, we would have additional counts. Sometimes a substantial fog set in around the area (which often delayed our morning routines); other times, one of the women would be missing (which is considered to be "out-of-bounds"). At counts, we were required to stand at our bunks, no exceptions. These counts allowed the unit officers to make sure each woman was accounted for. Not waking up for a count, not getting out of the shower in time for a count, or talking during a count, were infractions punishable with a trip to the SHU. Inane rules and the capricious consequences that followed became a daily occurrence. For example, one of my bunkies (and someone with whom I developed a close bond), was on a number of medications to treat her diagnosed psychotic disorders. These medications produced the unfortunate side effects of extreme lethargy and drowsiness. On several occasions, she had been sent to the hole for sleeping through daily counts (rule 320). What I found sad, although not completely surprising given our environment, was that her bunk mate at the time could have helped but refused to wake her up for the count.

> Sorry I haven't written much. I just got out of the fucking hole. A shot for petty shit makes me want to do some serious acting out . . . at least then I'd deserve it. It was an out-of-bounds shot [a disciplinary write-up for not being where you are supposed to be]. I'd gone to the dentist, had 2 teeth pulled, got all stitched up, and fell asleep. They called a senseless unscheduled count, and unbeknownst to me, I had a call-out to medical [a document from the medical staff, requesting to the see the inmate]. A fucking week in the hole and 30 days property restriction. Bullshit. (personal communication)

So much of my prison experience continues to stay with me; I felt emotionally crippled by all that I saw and all that I encountered. I slept with my eyes covered because of the interrogation-like lights being on at strange hours, unexpected flashlight "bed checks" from the guards, and a strong desire to ignore the various sexual exploits taking place around me. There is a hypersensitivity that develops while in prison, and it stays with a person for a substantial period of time. For close to two years after release, my body would tense up and I would get a queasy feeling in the pit of my stomach at 4 and 10 p.m.; I was able to tell time without ever looking at a clock.

I was in prison for a short time, and I cannot even imagine what it must be like for someone who serves a long term and the price their mind and bodies will pay upon release. There was so much chaos and activity; it was exhausting. Overstimulation led to an almost unbearable level of heightened responsiveness that ultimately followed me into my civilian life.

I find it interesting (sadly) that they make such a big deal
about our abuse histories (as part of our initial psych evals
when we first come in) and yet women are being emotionally, physically, sexually abused every day in here and outside on the compound. Where's the logic in that? (letter to
my brother)

CHICKEN-SHIT RULES

There were a variety of inane rules and regulations. Trying
to learn them all was nearly impossible, especially considering
they seemed to change depending on where you were and the
particular officer on duty. There seemed to be no rhyme or reason to most things in prison. The inconsistency of the decision
making was particularly frustrating (because something that
was allowable one day, would not be tolerated the next).

My travel plans to get back to Texas are fucked up for
another year or so because of my out-of-bounds shot—it
was a bullshit charge! A fucking week in the hole. . . . The
chickenshit rules change all the fucking time—especially at
quarterlies (rotation of guards into different units). The BOP
has also changed up their security point system making it
harder to transfer. We both know that the longer I wait, the
greater the chance I'll end up in trouble, thus starting this
crappy process all over again. (personal communication)

Almost everything in prison involves repetition—from our
daily preparations, to our dining hall habits and bathroom
schedules. Most prisoners find ways to fill their days; some are
more constructive than others. Idle time often seemed to be the
most painful, and it frightens me to think how years and
decades of time are filled (without going crazy). My routine
became something I looked forward to, and indeed found comfort in. How odd it must sound to others that the predictability
of the miserableness became comfortable. When my routine
was interrupted, I would find myself agitated, nervous, and
somewhat at a loss.

For the first portion of my sentence I would arrive at the
education center by call-out (7:30 a.m.), leave when dismissed
for lunch, and return to the school until roughly 3:30 p.m. We
were then sent back to our units for 4 p.m. count, mail call, and
then eventual release for dinner and evening activities. I often

skipped dinner and instead headed outside to the track for some exercise. It was important to get there early before it became crowded with the other women. The latter half of my sentence I had mornings off and would go into school following lunch, returning in the evenings. I preferred this schedule because it meant less time dealing directly with the women in the class-room. I also liked this schedule because it gave me more free-dom and quiet time to grade papers, read books, prepare lessons plans and the like, without the distraction from the many women who didn't want to be in school in the first place. Hav-ing my mornings off also meant I would have a more peaceful workout. It also meant less stress waiting for a shower and the hot water that was typically nonexistent by evenings.

By nature, I am not aggressive. I was generally the one to walk away from conflict rather than engage in an argument or stand my ground, which both have the potential for violence. I was both surprised and disgusted at the temper I sometimes displayed while I was locked up. Certainly, one can justify "get-ting tough" to avoid being seen as weak, but I suppose for some (myself included) there are just times when frustration and anger can't be kept inside. I was unsure where my rage came from, but there were times it did come out, and in those moments, each time felt right and justified. It was oddly cathar-tic. Sometimes it was about standing up for myself or another woman, while other times it was simply anxiety and fear that surfaced in very explosive ways.

> I threw my tray at her feet and stepped up to her. I was ter-rified but tried so hard to hide it. It felt like she was staring right through me. I couldn't move. She finally took a few steps back and told me I wasn't worth a shot (a disciplinary write-up). I moved even closer to her, not uttering a word. I was shocked (and grateful) she walked away. She definitely would have kicked my ass. Bad. The Lt was pissed and made me clean the mess, but I didn't care. The whole situa-tion made me sick to my stomach. I went back to my unit and threw up. I hate it here. (journal entry)

My first official misconduct came several weeks into my sentence, and it was for a rule infraction I did not know about. I had been running on the track and had the sleeves of my T-shirt rolled up, which was not allowed. An officer called me over to chastise me for "being stupid and not following the rules." Before I could stop myself, I responded with "You've got to be fucking kidding me!" Fortunately for me, he was not offended by my rebuttal; he simply admonished me, said next time it would be a shot, and waved me away with a dismissive flick of his wrist.

Much of what I've read in the corrections literature suggests that officers and prison officials are more inclined to let the little things go in favor of focusing on the bigger, more important issues. Not cracking down on all the frivolous rules and procedures provides the prisoner with a modicum of leeway; this is done in exchange for smoother running facilities and less hassle from the inmates. This did not seem to be the case in Tallahassee. It felt as if the little things were catastrophic occurrences, while major infractions like sexual assault and violence among the women were tolerated.

While the infractions might seem minor, punishment for them can have serious consequences. Research suggests that women are more likely than men to end up in solitary confinement for violations like disobedience. Discipline for small infractions can also result in the loss of opportunities like being able to buy food or hygiene supplies. Female prisoners often lose phone privileges or visitation rights. This is particularly problematic because more than 60% of women in state and federal prison have children under the age of 18 (Sentencing Project, 2019). Even more troubling is the loss of good time credits that many women lose from prison infractions. In California, between January 2016 and February 2018, women had the equivalent of 1,483 years added to their sentences through good credit revocations, and the rates were notably higher than for male prisoners (Shapiro, Pupovac, & Lydersen, 2018).

> I tried to go outside to the sports-oriented TV, but it really makes me want a beer—I must admit, this has been a great way to "go on the wagon," although there's booze around here if I really wanted it! Anyway, the women that hang out there typically do each other's hair, make out with each other, or fight with each other . . . none of which would bother me, *if I had a beer.* (letter to brother)

When the women leave the unit for the day, it is expected to be a certain way—bunks made, floors clean, lockers shut, etc. Contrary to condescending guards, and the belief that convicts are stupid, most women seem to understand the rules and regulations that govern prisons. While most units have laundry facilities (in addition to the laundry service for the entire prison), some of us preferred to hand wash our belongings, hanging them up or draping them to dry over night. My first official *shot* was for leaving one of my bras hanging from the back rail of my bunk. This was a punishable offense. It involved a frightening and humiliating visit to the lieutenant's office. Rather than informing me of my infraction and the punishment, I was called out of the education center, marched up to the main office (through the compound), and read my rights without being told what my "crime" had been. At this moment, there was no doubt in my mind where the power came from in this place, not that there ever really was any doubt.

> For our safety? Fuck that. They're in there telling us it's for our own safety—a fire drill in the fucking middle of the night—you know it was only because it was rainin'. It's fucking hurricane season, standing outside with nothing on in the pourin' rain. They just want us to know who's in charge, plus, you know it gave them a chance to shake us all down! (personal communication)

My penalty was a mark on my record and "assignment to hours of extra duty." It seemed ridiculous that the guards focused on such petty things, but perhaps it was more about trying to control the things they could. Scrutinizing the insignificant and the mundane appeared far more important than addressing the smoking, drinking, violence, or sexual activities that took place on a regular basis on the compound and within the units.

> You have staff here that are bothered with your presence even though they tell you to come see them. This makes absolutely no sense. They act like Dr. Jekyll and Mr. Hyde with you and it makes you question if it's actually you or if they are just bipolar. You also have the problem of learning the staff's individual rules, because none of them are consistent, in fact, nothing is consistent in this place except that most of the staff are completely moronic, which matches the personality of most of the inmates. (personal communication)

Chapter Four

The Pains of Imprisonment

Prior to my own legal issues, I was a punitive, get-tough employee of the justice system. My prison experience opened my eyes to the reality of the administration, application, and implementation of judicial processes in this country. I have spent much of the last few years critiquing my earlier convictions, trying to place those ideals in the present, to make sense of them through the lens of new experiences.

> We didn't get toilet paper again this week—can you imagine running low on tp, tampons and pads at a women's prison? Really? Except for the older gals, it wouldn't surprise me a bit if we were all cycling our periods together. Nasty. We ran low a couple of weeks ago while we were in the midst of the whole riot thing (their symbolic show of force, having the SWAT teams running around here tossing smoke bombs and shooting off pellet guns, showing us who's boss. Yup, they showed us.). Not getting tp this week was probably more due to officer laziness! I've never seen such laziness. I did manage to "borrow" some stuff from the school . . . a bunch of women out right stole a lot of these things from other places and other people. (journal entry)

Despite the huge expenditure of state and federal dollars on the construction of high-tech facilities, jails and prisons in the United States remain neglected and vicious institutions (Shelden & Veléz, 2020). The atrocious and harsh treatment is the intended result of get-tough, no-frills penal values articulated by some of our country's most influential policy makers. Our vengeful penal philosophy has led to an offensive level of cruelty and human rights abuses, many of which remain largely below the public radar. The first quotation below is from a woman 3 months into her 12-year sentence for a nonviolent drug crime. Her comment was echoed by a number of female convicts sharing similar experiences.

> This [in a discussion about conditions in Federal facilities] is nothing, you should see the fucked up way they treat us in County. People are threatened and raped all the time, but nobody gives a shit 'cuz we're animals. Our words don't mean anything, you can complain all you want; your word against the guards, all that does is get you beat down even more. Get this man, on the outside what we have to say means shit, but by God if you can provide the feds with information about another crime or another criminal [referring to a "rule 35"—which allows the courts to reduce an offender's sentence if they can provide "substantial assistance" to the government], our words are gold. How fucked up is that? (personal communication)

> The visit from my husband was wonderful and I managed to survive the strip search—how positively humiliating. He visited for three days. He is having a very hard time and working to find out more about the "second chance" bill that is before the senate. It appears that I would be a perfect candidate for it [meeting all the qualifications for participation]. I'd love to be closer to home. It's crazy that there is a camp near _____ [prisoner's hometown], and I'm a first-time offender (also nonviolent)—it just doesn't make any sense. I know I'm one of the lucky ones, so few have family that can actually afford to travel. (personal communication)

Prisons are a central component in the criminal justice system in the United States. We have always relied heavily on incarceration as a sanction for criminal behavior. However, an examination of the nation's history reveals substantial variations in public attitudes toward convicted felons. Periods of liberal reform are correlated with support for the enlightened treatment of prisoners and the upgrading of prison conditions, in less liberal times, the opposite is true.

Over the years, both prisons and jails have employed a variety of punitive and barbaric techniques with the sole purpose of revenge. They also exemplify a tendency to use punishment for its own end, with no regard for potential rehabilitation (Kappeler & Potter, 2018). This intolerance is reflected in the harsher prison sentences meted out to offenders in recent years. As incarceration rates have increased, living conditions in prisons and jails have deteriorated. Furthermore, the availability of rehabilitation programs has decreased as the system struggles simply to accommodate the increased prisoner volume. Legislators continue to publicize their attempts to intensify the pains of imprisonment by reducing such inmate amenities as grants for college education, television privileges, computers in cells, and exercise through weight lifting

As the next several passages indicate, the majority of the women in prison are well aware of the disconnect that exists between the system's illusion of "correcting" offenders, and the reality of opportunities and survival after release.

> Rehabilitation. . . . I don't think I even know what the fuck that is. It's not that I don't know sellin' drugs is illegal, but what the hell else am I 'sposed to do? If I could change my life, don't you 'spose I'd do it? Do them legal people actually think this is a world I would choose . . . fuck that, it's called survival. Lock my ass up, that's fine, but I'm gettin' out, and I still can't read, I still can't get and keep a job, I still got babies to support, and I still can't find a decent place to live cuz I got no money and now I got a record, what the fuck else they think I'm gonna do? (personal communication)

> The jobs and programs seem worthless. I'm not sure how they expect this to prepare these women for reentry to the general workforce, I might agree if we were traveling back in time with plans to reenter somewhere around the 1930s. The only things that are accomplished with the current model is that the FBOP gets cheap labor. (personal communication)

> I think I'd like to go back to school, but let's face it, I'm not that smart! I do want to better myself. Lord knows my achievements in life have been few, but the ones I've had felt good. I'm determined not to pass down my bad choices, and being poor, and living day to day, I don't want that for my kids. (personal communication)

Upon release, many female prisoners face daunting obstacles (Sawyer, 2018). They must find a job that will provide an income, as well as something that will afford them a modicum of emotional and psychological support. Without this, the released convict depends on welfare or engages in illegal activity to fulfill her needs, as well as the needs of her children. Effective programs geared towards the training of offenders are crucial if offenders are to succeed post-prison. Considering that so many of our prisoners are locked up for nonviolent crime, it seems to me that the country's incarceration binge is doing far more harm than good.

WHY WOULD WE EXPECT ANYTHING DIFFERENT?

Mass incarceration combined with a shift in the overall demographic makeup of the prison population of the United States have given rise to an exceedingly malevolent prison culture. Unyielding crime policies and Draconian sentencing laws have expanded the prison population at exorbitant and unmanageable rates. The War on Drugs has not only increased the size of our prison population, but also has heavily skewed the population mix toward society's marginalized individuals and people of color (Shelden & Vasiliev, 2018). Arrests, convictions, and incarceration rates differ drastically among socioeconomic sectors and racial groups in the United States. The prison system is filled with people who do not have a quality education and have historically been shut out of good jobs.

The vast majority of those in the criminal justice system were either impoverished or among the working poor at the time of their arrest. The median pre-prison income ($19,185) of incarcerated people was 41% lower than the median income ($32,517) of non-incarcerated people; the median pre-prison income of imprisoned women was $13,890 (Rabuy & Kopf, 2015).

> Our society has, in the name of being tough on crime, made a series of policy choices that have fueled a cycle of poverty and incarceration. We send large numbers of people with low levels of education and low skills to prison, and then when they leave just as penniless as they were when they went in, we expect them to bear the burden of legally-acceptable employment discrimination. (p. 3)

Penal policies have moved away from the basic principles that correctional services must be effectual, accountable, and humane. Spurred by the tough-on-crime rhetoric marketed by political officials seeking public support, a mentality has developed that endorses punitive treatment. The attitude is that criminals deserve whatever they get; punishment should be painful (Kappeler & Potter, 2018). Todd Clear (1994) described the increased punitiveness in the treatment of prisoners since

1973 as *penal harm*. He and Natasha Frost (2014) refer to punitive penal policies as the *punishment imperative* that emerged
from a general alarm about crime before coalescing into a
broader narrative about crime and justice.

> U.S. penal policies grew steadily and inexorably toward an
> ever-harder edge. Thresholds of punitiveness people never
> thought our democracy would ever have to confront
> became a part of official policy: life without parole and
> death penalties for young people; lengthy detention before
> trial; humiliation and long periods of extreme isolation dur-
> ing confinement; decades behind bars for minor thefts and
> possession of drugs. Such developments would have been
> unthinkable in the 1960s, but they would become the lead-
> ing edge of penal reform in the years that followed. (p. 2)

In 2016, there were 2,162,400 people incarcerated in our
prisons and jails (Kaeble & Cowhig, 2018). Intolerable, inhu-
mane, and unacceptable conditions include unnecessary and
degrading strip searches, food that is sometimes rotten or marginal in nutritious value, as well as the denial of medical care,
medications, and mental health treatment.

> Those convicted of serious crimes must be punished and
> imprisoned—knowing that imprisonment itself is very
> punitive; we need not punish above and beyond imprison-
> ment. This means that we need not and must not degrade,
> provoke, nor excessively deprive the human beings we have
> placed there. (Irwin, 1980, p. 248)

The prison complex has become an ominous presence in
our society to an extent unmatched in our history. Most people
know very little about the current state of crime and punishment in America. "They are continually bombarded with the
myths, misconceptions, and half-truths that dominate public
discussion" (Currie, 2013, p. 4). The truths are often hidden or
buried, ignored as the complaints of coddled criminals sorry
and remorseful only because they were caught. "The public sen-
timent for harsh treatment of people who break the law
remains deeply seated in the political mind and social character
of the nation," although the get-tough movement has lost some
of its salience with the public because crime has been dropping
nationally over a number of years (Clear & Frost, p. 4).

Research has shown that prisoners who maintain close contact with their families have lower rates of recidivism (Santo,

2017). Many of the women I met in prison were confined hundreds of miles away from children, family, and friends. They were impeded from contacts known to promote and encourage a more positive and crime-free lifestyle upon release. The following comments were from two women serving lengthy sentences at FCI Tallahassee at great distances away from their families.

> How am I supposed to maintain a relationship with my kids when the feds ship me 800 miles away? How am I 'sposed to be a mom? My kids won't know me when I get out. Not only am I being punished, but my kids are being punished too. They want to give me classes on how to be a better momma, but I can't see my own babies! How is it good to have State people taking care of my babies? (personal communication)

> I can't fucking believe the time has finally come! It's about time they send my ass back to Texas—there's no need to be this far away from my family. I've been down too long and it isn't right. My parents are stressed with all the business—4 grand kids, 2 great grand, and 2 significant others in 1 house can cause lots of problems. I know my mom will be glad I'm closer to them and the kids. I'm looking forward to the first visit; I'm going to be nervous though. It's been over 2 years since I've seen my parents/kiddos—fucking ridiculous! How do the feds get away with keeping us so far away from the things that motivate us the most? (personal communication)

Two other women who had been transferred to facilities closer to their families described their feelings.

> I had a really great visit last weekend. Both my mom and my dad came, and even my two girls and the baby. They all looked so happy and healthy, except mom. She's getting older, but she's still sharp as a tack. I can't believe I had gone as long as I did without seeing them, that's the worst punishment of all. It's not as painful to see them go now, because deep down, you know you'll see them again. (personal communication)

> My family was here a couple of weeks ago. Needless to say, I've been highly depressed. I wish I was high, I'd rather feel numb then the ache in my heart I feel watching my kids walk away. The visit was long overdue. Everyone looked great. It's been years since we got to hold each other. The jails I've been in are all behind glass, and that fucks with

> your head let me tell you. It was just so sad to watch them
> leave. I practically kicked them out just to spare us all the
> weeping. I'm finally feeling better; it seemed like I was cry-
> ing all the time there for a while—talk about looking weak,
> I was a mess! (personal communication)

My experience within the walls of FCI Tallahassee aligns
with the research that most women are sentenced for nonviolent crimes such as fraud or drug-related offenses (Pollock,
2014). However, any attempt to characterize female offenders
must be hedged by disclaimers, as no single description can capture the variety of etiologies, traits, susceptibilities, or sheer
randomness of influences that impel people to violate the law. I
would suggest that the typical female offender, being nonwhite,
poor, and a single parent, is repeatedly victimized by society.
She is expected to work to support herself and her children and
to be a good parent. When she finds these expectations impossible to fulfill and resorts to crime, she is punished. There is no
assistance with family care or medical expenses. She is caught
in an unwinnable situation.

Most of the women I encountered came from poverty, were
addicted to drugs or alcohol, and had emotional or mental
health problems. My bunkie, for example, suffered from depression and schizophrenia. She had been violently raped as a teen-
ager, dropped out of high school, and spent time living on the
streets. She was a prostitute with a severe drug and alcohol
addiction who clumsily robbed banks to support her addictions,
her disabled schizophrenic mother, her two children (from two
different unsupportive fathers), her drug-addicted younger
brother, and the pimp who beat her on a regular basis. She was
23 at the time that we met. Her crimes, like many, were a
response to crisis and long-standing disadvantage. The money
she earned was the primary source of family income. I am by
no means suggesting that these circumstances excuse her criminal behavior, but they should certainly help to explain it. She
explained her life as follows.

> Sure I tried to work real jobs, but something always came
> up and I got fired or I had to quit. My mom was real sick,
> and if she didn't get her meds, she couldn't take care of my
> kids. I was making minimum wage and it felt like I was
> working only enough to pay for medical stuff for my
> babies and rent to keep us all off the streets. It's not like I

woke up one morning and decided that turning tricks was the answer, but my babies' daddies didn't help none. Society has put out there all these things people should strive for, except not all of us get the same chances to get there. (personal communication)

Another woman commented.

I've been a prostitute for years; I've been beaten, raped, and sold . . . but I fed my kids and I had a place for my momma to live. Nobody never wanted to help me then, but now all of a sudden they want to lock me up. It ain't my priorities that need to change, it's how to keep those priorities and not be killed in the meantime. (personal communication)

Many of the women I met struggled to recognize the patterns of violence and addiction, while also acknowledging the cycle of abuse and generational poverty that plagued their families. For most, their crimes were not committed to *avoid* legitimate jobs or careers, but rather *in response to* years of desperation and depravation. Otherwise decent women engaged in criminal behavior to survive in neighborhoods and communities ravaged by deteriorating schools, the decline of local businesses, and the loss of job opportunities.

The women I spent time with were devoted to their children. Many lined their lockers with pictures, cards, and letters. As we settled into our units in the evenings, their bunks would be strewn with photographs. They talked about their loved ones with tears in their eyes, and with pride at the accomplishments of those on the outside. But I could also see fear and uncertainty as they attempted to care for a child so far away, and with so little contact. Some of the women expressed helplessness as they readily admitted that their children were showing signs of trouble—dropping out and/or failure in school, spending time with delinquent peers or engaging in gang activity, contact with law enforcement, and experimenting with drugs and alcohol. Many children were living with grandparents or distant relatives; their fathers were equally likely to be in prison.

There were so many stories of abuse and addiction, and of children being taken away—becoming permanent fixtures of the welfare and criminal justice systems. Many of the women were frustrated and deeply saddened that their children were wards of the state. Children of imprisoned women are five times more likely to end up in foster care than the children of imprisoned men (Hager & Flagg, 2018). Regardless of the seriousness of the offense committed, 1 in 8 will lose parental rights. The Adoption and Safe Families Act of 1987 mandated that federally funded state child-welfare programs must begin termination of parental rights of children who had been in foster care for 15 of the previous 22 months. A few states have implemented some relief for incarcerated parents. Dorothy Roberts, an expert on family law at the University of Pennsylvania, comments that the underlying problem in the child-welfare system is the bias against poor parents by decision makers—especially against incarcerated mothers of color.

I'd spent years reading about and studying the criminal justice system, but the impact on people caught in the system was never the focus. Now when I study the literature and explore the topic with my students, I am struck by the lack of humanity offenders are given. In books and media accounts, criminals are blank, devoid of human characteristics. I remember sitting in my bunk listening to the many and varied women as they told their stories. I could not help but be drawn into their worlds—worlds I vaguely understood, although some people and situations still find their way into my dreams. At times I found myself involved in their lives. To live with these women in such close proximity initially meant a forced involvement. What seemed awkward and uncomfortable at first, eventually became a source of solace, binding us together. All that I had read about and studied eventually meant nothing as I spent my time living, learning, and growing with these women.

Official data means little in prison. Instead the faces, the lives, the stories, and even the deaths are what matters. People give these stories meaning.

> For me it is a struggle to remember who I am . . . and to not allow myself to be degraded just because I made a mistake. Everyone does. That is not who I am or who we are. I don't want to become the person the criminal justice system says I am. (personal communication)

What you read in most published accounts of crime, whether in textbooks or newspaper articles (or broadcast on television), paints a black and white picture of right and wrong (us versus them). What I saw and experienced was very different. I saw generations of abuse, poverty, frustration, and social isolation. Few of the women were lazy or stupid. Many have lost sight of priorities and responsibilities, the effects of addiction and love in relationships that hurt or come with a price.

> I know society thinks I'm a bad mother, and that I don't love my babies, but that's just not true. I loved them so much I simply lost sight of the "right" way to take care of them. It makes me angry that people think that just because we're criminals that we don't feel loss and hurt or love and pride—as if committing a crime doesn't make me human anymore. (personal communication)

I was also surprised by the number of women I met who had been involved and sentenced as "coconspirators." The image of the offender painted by society has us all lumped together as violent predators (or perhaps the black-widow type of woman who kills her spouse portrayed on *Snapped*). But the crimes committed by the women I met were as varied and diverse as the women themselves. Some, like me, had made a conscious choice without being under the influence of any mind-altering substances. Others could not remember the crimes they committed, sometimes aware of what happened only through police reports and details related by family and friends.

Many cases involved women responding to (and fighting back) in domestic violence situations. I really was stunned at the number of women who had been the victim of spousal and intimate partner abuse. Some were convicted for killing their partners; others had hired a hit man. At the time of my release, two of the women I had been working with had "murder for hire" convictions. Both were interesting cases, and both women seemed "normal" by all standards and accounts. I enjoyed working with them. The thing that struck me most was how *average* many of these women were—physically, intellectually, socially, etc. Despite media accounts, the typical female offender is indeed quite ordinary.

For many women their crimes were connected to the men in their lives. Some of the women admitted to trying to cover up the crimes committed by their men. Others were "set-up" when their man turned on them—seeking a reduced sentence and/or blaming the women for whatever crimes had been committed. Interestingly enough, I did meet some women who had turned their partners in as part of their sentencing deals; however, those circumstances were fairly rare.

MAINLINE TO THE SHAKEDOWN SHACK

Make no mistake, a significant number of the women I met belonged in prison. I have struggled, though, with how I think society should respond. On the one hand, I want to be critical of the federal government for warehousing and perpetuating the cycle of violence and despair. On the other hand, I came into contact with women who were predatory and dangerous. I strongly believe they should not be wandering freely in society.

The majority of the women I met in prison, however, were quite kind and caring toward one another. However, there was also constant bickering, arguing, fighting, and blatant displays of brutality that often overshadowed the friendships and loving relationships.

> [Inmate's name] threatened to kick my ass today, God I hate this place! I was in the dining hall, when it all went down. I wish A. and P. had been there, although I'm not sure it would have changed anything. I was scared to death but was more scared about simply walking away from her . . . *so I didn't.* (journal entry)

Dealing with the internal strife and the constant conflict was exhausting, but this discord was probably indicative of the lives many of these women lived outside the prison walls. To be sure, the first fight I witnessed, the first time I saw a sexually aggressive/violent act, the first time I observed somebody putting body fluids in the food, and the constant reign of terror from some officers were undeniably jarring to me. All of these things deeply impacted me, but I struggled most with the cacophony of noises, day in and day out. It never stopped; it was never quiet. The inability to escape the pandemonium and the chaos was the most difficult aspect of prison life for me. Without any peace, there's never really time to make sense of all that goes on, to interpret or digest the experiences, or to put them into perspective relative to the women and the personal characteristics and lifestyle choices that landed them in prison.

Each and every day, sometimes twice a day, the staff, guards, and/or administration would line up outside the dining hall. This "mainline" was a designated time that allowed inmates to approach prison personnel to ask questions or to seek help. The women found this insincere and insulting; to us it seemed only a symbolic display of concern. Mainline felt hollow, a futile exercise of shuffling blame from prison official to prison administrator (and back again)—much like the bureaucracy I experienced before I was incarcerated. Questions were rarely answered. When they were, it generally meant seeing another administrative person.

Resolution to our problems was rare. Issues raised during the mainline included: destroyed mail (if we got it at all), phone calls routinely cut off in mid conversation, money never deposited to our accounts, abusive treatment by the guards, complaints about discipline violations (shots), the lack of follow-up for medical requests, and loved ones (including the elderly and very young children) spending hours in the heat, the rain, and the cold waiting for visitation hours that at times were cancelled with no warning and no notice. Seldom was any action taken by the prison personnel. Certainly not all prison complaints are valid, but even the simplest requests were ignored. The pretentious display of inmate support made us feel even more insignificant.

The dining hall is actually an interesting, albeit initially frightening place. At first blush it could be a cafeteria in a strip mall or on a college campus. There are people frantically running about and lines of women waiting to be herded around like cattle. The first thing one sees are the uniforms, khaki everywhere! Despite vastly different ages, races, and ethnicities, we all look eerily similar as we have all been stripped of our individuality and uniqueness. Inside the dining hall there is a constant clamor that rises above all else, you can hear specific names being called out, just as you hear the commanding voices of certain guards as they direct and supervise the area. As with most things in prison, there is a great deal of time spent waiting—the dining hall was no exception. It takes a while to become familiar with the labyrinth of hot food rows, the beverage line, or the surprisingly decent salad bar. For brief moments, it was easy to forget we are in prison. The meals, for the most part, were good, southern comfort food at its best. To be fair, there really was no reason for anyone to go hungry, particularly when you include the food products that could be purchased from the commissary, as well as the food regularly taken from the dining hall and stored in various hiding places across the institution.

Pregnant women and those with medical conditions such as diabetes were allowed to go to the dining hall first. Interestingly enough, our most feared Lieutenant appeared to have a soft spot for these women, as she went out of her way to accommodate them (it was rare to see this side of her, but at times, it did make her almost tolerable). The units were let out in a very specific order. Each week, the units were inspected; this included bunks being made, floors being mopped, bathrooms cleaned, and the like. We were "rated" best to worst, and the designation earned determined the order in which units could enter the dining hall. G unit, notorious for being clean and getting some of the highest inspection marks, typically went to the dining hall first. It was so strange that such a simple reward as getting to leave your unit first was an incredible motivator for most. It inspired many to "assist" others in cubicle and unit chores. The ranking extended beyond who would be allowed to eat first. Higher ranked units also were first in line for the commissary or specific activities out on the compound.

My Thanksgiving meal shattered some preconceptions. The dining hall was unusually crowded that afternoon. The guards were particularly edgy. The women were loud; the quarters were cramped, and I was feeling exceptionally sad and anxious. I generally ate my meals with the same 2 or 3 women, but the limited space forced us to sit wherever we could find a chair. I ultimately ended up "sharing" my meal with three women serving lengthy sentences for varying degrees of homicide. Sitting across from me was a was a bitter, inhospitable, and loud Dominican woman sentenced to 200+ years for killing her infant, eviscerating the corpse, stuffing it full of drugs, and trying to cross the borders of this country. She made no attempt to hide her feelings of disdain and resentment at having to eat with us rather than her usual cohort. This was not my first encounter with her; I disliked her immensely. The woman next to me had received a life sentence for her part in a string of murders; she had been incarcerated for about 16 years of multiple consecutive life-sentences. She and her female partner committed the homicides while working in a nursing home in the Midwest. This lady would later become a tutor, working with me daily at the education center. She was nice and incredibly bright. Across from her at the table was a woman serving two life sentences for homicides. She was a pretty woman, petite in

stature, and soft spoken. Her murders allegedly had been committed for profit.

Generally, I found that women convicted of the most violent and destructive crimes were the most pleasant and the eas-
iest women to be around. Perhaps it was their ability to keep
their rage under the surface that allowed them to interact in the
general population without drawing much attention. I should
temper my description about the regularity of aggression that
takes place in prison by stating that most of the women simply
want to do their time with as little conflict as possible. Most
female inmates are not true members of the convict culture—
norms, values, and belief systems that typically govern prisoner behavior (for example, "pay your debts," "do your own
time," "don't be a snitch," etc.). Many women prisoners do not
subscribe to the convict culture's rules for living. Most of the
women I came into contact with merely wanted to get along in
prison without trouble, and many of them had hopes of "going
straight" upon release.

For many women, the experiences of arrest and conviction
are enough to deter future criminality. One woman contem-
plates the "cost" of her crime, explaining to me that the process
of going through the system was punishment enough.

> It ain't worth it! All that money I stole, I pissed it away and
> had nothing to show for it. Now I'm in here, my family
> hates me, I'm not sure I can go back to my hometown, I'll
> probably never find a job, all this shame and embarrass-
> ment. But really, all the feds had to do was arrest me and
> put my name in the paper—I didn't need to come here to
> prison, to be beat down, or to see what I've seen—I'd never
> commit another crime just from all the stuff that happened
> to me before I got here. (personal communication)

The serial killer/tutor, for example, was at times a bit
"spooky," but in an interesting way. I was caught off guard by
how much I enjoyed talking with her. Perhaps it was my background and education in forensic psychology that drew me to
her, or, as my brother pointed out, maybe we got along because
she and I were both fascinated with the macabre. My interest
was, of course, academic; spending time with her on a personal
level allowed me to view her "mask of sanity" up close and personal. She was articulate and witty, with a very peculiar (but
funny) sense of humor. Sometimes our classes would be can-

celled. Although the students were not required to be there, the tutors still had to show up at the school to grade papers, clean out files, and finish up various chores on our "to do" list. When our work was completed, we had free time; we could read, type letters, and even watch movies.

Sometimes the other tutors and I would watch a movie together, typically an old black and white classic. The conversations that followed these great movies were interesting and thoughtful, and I often found myself feeling somewhat less anxious about where I was and with *whom*. As much as I have criticized society and mainstream media about its portrayal of convicts, I was also guilty of a distorted perception. My experience in prison changed a number of things for me, not the least of which was my own idea about what it meant to be a criminal (convict).

> I "acquired" a bootleg copy of a book written about one of the serial killers in here! Crazy, right? It's amazing what a convict can get if truly motivated! (I can't believe I just said that!) I had to put a makeshift book cover over it in case someone got nosey. It's pretty good (considering the topic), but bits and pieces are difficult to read. I don't read it before I go to bed! (letter to my brother)

APATHY IN SUFFERING

As one would expect, many of the women seemed to experience a broad range of emotions, some moment to moment, others day to day. As previously mentioned, emotions often floated just below the surface, and the unpredictable nature of the place was exhausting, as the mood or tenor of the afternoon could change in a flash. It is difficult to put into words, but there was an undeniable "feel" to the institution. We could tell when something was "in the air." The atmosphere would change—and there would be a sensation such as when the hair stands up on the back of your neck, or that uneasy feeling in the pit of your stomach. As prisoners we developed a hypersensitive coping mechanism; we were particularly attuned to our surroundings. This sense of hypervigilance was arduous.

There were times I felt a sense of peace and acceptance, an uncanny calm that swept over the facility. Without warning, there could be an explosion of resentment and anger that gripped and embraced each of us, a volatile reminder of where we were and the rage of people around us. Sometimes this shift was predictable—a shakedown, a fight, or some other serious event. At other times, it was subtle, a combustible combination of depression, guilt, and anger—at ourselves, at our captors, at life as a whole.

> I missed lunch today (not that *that* is any real loss), but I missed it because the "mail room" (and I use that term loosely) is open 1 hour a day about twice a week and I needed to ask a couple of questions. Not knowing they couldn't send cash or a book of stamps, 2 of my friends sent the items. The mail room is supposed to put a slip of paper (documenting the item and telling the inmate it's being returned to sender) in the envelope with a signature and a date. Neither of the letters I received had that slip of paper, so I went to ask, simply for clarification. The guy just looks at me and says he can't find any paperwork stating the items were received or sent back! He simply says, "I don't know what to tell you, I'm not the only guy who works back here . . . the mail room is not accountable for those things"—what the hell? Not accountable? What the fuck is wrong with these people? I ranted and raved for awhile, but knew I didn't want a shot over this, so I walked away and chalked it up to how this place functions overall. I think the thing that gets me most is that it's one thing for the staff to treat us convicts like garbage, but it's yet another thing to treat outsiders like that—completely unacceptable. (letter to my brother)

While facility and unit inspections were daily routines, the staff and administration were even more oppressive when higher authorities were scheduled to visit the prisons. According to the Bureau of Prisons, there are 6 regional offices that provide oversight and technical assistance to the facilities located in their respective regions. FCI Tallahassee is part of the southeast region, which covers 6 states. The regional office provided supervision to 23 government-run institutions, 3 private prisons, and 4 residential reentry (RRM) field offices (Federal Bureau of Prisons, 2019).

The American Correctional Association (ACA) is a private, nonprofit organization largely composed of current and former corrections officials. It provides accreditation to prisons, jails, and other detention facilities. FCI Tallahassee is an ACA accredited facility. The ACA develops the standards that are supposed to enhance how the correctional institution operates for the benefit of all those involved (inmates, staff, and administration). Prison standards are established by the ACA, often with no oversight by government agencies (Friedman, 2014). The accreditation process is basically a paper review; there is no regular on-site monitoring of the facilities. The ACA role is to substantiate whether a facility has policies that comply with the standards. Some prisons have experienced significant problems despite being accredited. For example, the Otter Creek Correctional Center in Kentucky, operated by Corrections Corporation of America (CCA), was accredited by the ACA in 2009 when at least five prison employees were prosecuted for raping and sexually abusing prisoners. Several states withdrew their female prisoners from Otter Creek following the sex scandal, but the facility did not lose its accreditation. The prison has since closed.

> Regional is coming—we're so overcrowded in here. They make us move the bunkbeds out of the hallways and television rooms. It makes us wonder if they send us from unit to unit just ahead of regional so they won't see everyone congregated together. (journal entry)

> Things are finally starting to settle down here. Week before last we had an ACA inspection that they made a whole insane hoopla about! Kind-of like when Regional comes × 100. . . . You remember that fucking train wreck I'm sure. Yet again we power-washed the inside of the coolers and the warehouse, scrubbed and painted—it was madness on the compound. All work crews were working overtime and weekends. Then, when the big day comes—NOTHING! It felt like one big set-up. They barely looked at anything! And then they passed this broke down mother-fucker! Passed! Are you kidding me? (personal correspondence)

I recalled a conversation I had with a colleague (and friend) shortly after my release about the damages done to those in prison. It struck me that most people in society probably believe that prisoners who are not beaten or abused (however one wants to define *abuse*) will be "just fine" when they return to society. But I often wonder, "Am I fine?" Do emotional scars go far deeper than the physical scars? What about the constant verbal put-downs, the torment, the daily reminders of how small and insignificant we are? How is that damaged assessed, and is it really any less important than physical abuse?

> Have you been to the fucking upper compound? The fuck-ers are marching around the perimeter of the compound with a cadence song " . . . look to your right what do you see, I see female inmates staring back at me." (personal communication)

> You definitely have to look at the issue of who is tending this adult day care—It has been my personal experience that, other than the education department, that most of the guards and officers have little compassion or even care in the least for the inmates. I don't understand how our unit team can be expected to give their opinions on our progress, when, in my own case, neither my counselor nor my unit manager have spent more than 10 minutes with me in the past 6 months. I find their 6-month team meetings to be an insult. How they have the nerve to judge my progress when they don't even know my name. (personal communication)

Chapter Five

Life on the Compound

The activity on the compound was as varied as the women that filled its walls. I met women from all walks of life. Somehow, we all had to learn to adapt to our new environment. It is a world like no other, and each day (and night) brought something new. Prison reality is indeed harsh and unrelenting, with a hidden culture of norms, values, and social roles not seen on the outside. The milieu forced us to think only about surviving day to day. Hope was almost nonexistent, although subtle glimmers of what *could be* permeated the walls, creating visions of a life not lived.

> Some young poor white girl tried to kill herself the other day by jumping from the roof of the chapel—she lived, but they say she's pretty fucked up. (personal communication)

For many, to have hope for, or to dream of, a better life would just make time that much more painful. I would only be there for a short time, but the weight of my future was heavy and oppressive. I was certain that if I could not shut off that dread of a constricted future, I would surely be crushed to death. I had to survive now, and that meant I had to learn to reconcile myself to prison life, to the immediacy of the violence and the bedlam, as well as the mundane and the monotonous.

> If I stare hard enough through the fence and the razor wire, it seems to disappear. What I wouldn't give to be somewhere else. . . . Tonight, like so many, my thoughts were interrupted by yelling, streams of profanity, the frenzied sounds of gravel under steel-toed shoes, and the unmistaken sound of bodies coming together violently, with force, and with anger. The perimeter guard shouts to the women, pointing his rifle. The blaring compound speaker

comes on and admonishes all of us to go back to our units. Another day ends just as chaotically as it started. There is predictability in the miserableness. (journal entry)

Barely 8 a.m. and already a couple of gals are headed to the hole for fighting—good God. One of the gals was supposed to leave soon, but this shot will knock off about 12 days of good time. (journal entry)

Evenings on the compound were most often a welcome break from the monotony of the day. I suppose on some level the women here were lucky. We had a certain amount of free time. Within certain limitations, we could entertain ourselves as we saw fit. Some women would be seated at the tables, playing cards or dominoes, while others sat crocheting or working on various craft projects. Cigarette smoke wafted up from corners of the compound (the facility became nonsmoking after I left). One could hear laughter and yelling as women celebrated birthdays (their own, or of distant children or loved ones) or anniversaries missed. There were times the workout center looked more like an outdoor picnic area. Women could be seen walking or running on the track, playing on the basketball courts, or doing aerobics with a group of others. While many women tried to make the best of their free time, others used the time to confront someone who had wronged them earlier in the day. It was not uncommon to see violent confrontations for debts not paid or transgressions in a relationship. If these outbursts got out of hand, we would all be sent back to our units and were locked up for the night. I was astonished when I realized that some women actually did this on purpose. If they were unhappy, they needed to make sure everyone else was equally as unhappy.

Commissary night was a time all its own. Despite the price-gouging, outdated products, sometimes spoiled snacks, and the extraordinarily long waits in line (often in the rain), it was often the highlight of the week. For many of us, it represented an opportunity not only to visit with friends and get out of our units, but also a chance to feel somewhat normal in the ability to purchase items that mildly reminded us of freedom and life on the outside. For some women it was something simple like hair color or plain white T-shirts; for others it was envelopes and pens/pencils. My girlfriends and I would splurge for ice cream once in awhile, as there's little better on a hot muggy Florida evening.

Commissary supplies vary greatly from facility to facility; what would be allowed in one place would be considered contraband in another. At FCI Tallahassee, one could buy anything from arts and craft supplies to fruits and sweets, an amazing selection. There was a wide variety of toiletry items, medical supplies such as aspirin and antihistamines, beauty supplies such as shampoo and make-up, and even a variety of foods like fruit or candy. We were each given a specific night of the week (based on our prison ID number) when we could go "shopping." And while it is very easy to complain and to criticize the lack of sundries and various comforts of home, I must admit, it felt incredibly good to simply *have* a sliver of normalcy, a reminder of life on the outside.

As I gradually became more accustomed to my surroundings (I would hesitate to say I was ever really comfortable), I was able to venture out to the various areas of the facility. The compound alternated between "open" and "closed" at various intervals throughout the day and you could only be outside when it was open. You could essentially go anywhere. If the compound closed, you had to remain where you were until the compound reopened. I was genuinely surprised at all that was offered, particularly in terms of recreation activities and equipment. At the far outskirts of the institution was a large track. As mentioned previously, I spent much of my free time there. There was a city park just down from the perimeter, and in the evening you could hear children laughing, baseball games being played, and whistles and buzzers blaring across the fields. The sounds were wonderful, and I think that was why I was originally drawn to the area.

Depending on the time of day, a certain amount of solitude could be found. Unfortunately, one was far more likely to witness fights and sexual transgressions than to spend time in quiet contemplation. Just beyond the track there was a volleyball pit (complete with sand), a basketball court, a baseball diamond, a weight and nautilus area, and an outside viewing television (under a picnic-type structure). This TV "was restricted to sports or sports news" at all times! There were racquetball tournaments on the weekends. It really was amazing. It almost looked like a college campus, with the exception of the rows and rows of razor wire, and the guard in the truck patrolling the compound perimeter.

THE PATIO

The highlight of my day was the time spent on "the patio" (the cement stoops that lined the compound) with friends. Here I experienced some of my most intense connections to others. Sometimes we sat in comfortable silence; other times we shared with each other our journeys through life. We discussed, almost dissected, our lives prior to prison. We recounted stories of pain and unimaginable sorrow and loss, our lessons of love, of resourcefulness and forgiveness, the necessity of laughter, our courage to take risks, and our willingness to fight for those things in which we believed the most. This emotional cleansing, with women so very different from me (or anyone I knew), helped heal old wounds. It seems so strange now as I look back, remembering the past with new insight and appreciation for all that I have learned.

> I was out on the track today, in my own world as usual, when L. came running up behind me and mockingly jumped on my back. We laughed and hugged, and recanted stories of the day. We listened to music on our portable radios, made fun of each other's dancing abilities, and shared stories about loved ones in our lives. How is it in a world so far away I find companionship and emotional freedom like nothing I've ever experienced? Is it because all the superficial bullshit means nothing here? Is it because degradation and humiliation have stripped away our exteriors? Is it because we share an experience that has so profoundly changed us? (journal entry)

> Sitting with P. on the patio, I can almost forget where I am. I awoke to the usual fighting and screaming—God I hate the hollering. I made my bunk, fixed my coffee, and wandered outside knowing she would be there. The anxiety dissipates with a friendly wave and a comforting smile. Today, like many, we discuss failure. She has been here 6 years, and I think how lucky she must be—she doesn't seem to fear failure, but rather seems to embrace it. (journal entry)

ARRIVAL OF THE SHIPMENTS

A shipment of 30+ came in tonight; Lord knows where they are going to put them. They've already got bunks/

cots stacked up in the TV room and in the hallway. (journal entry)

The arrival of new shipments (slang term for inmates) took a variety of forms. An inmate who self-surrenders, as I did, enters the compound in an entirely different uniform. You must stay in this outfit for a day or two until standard issue prison wear can be assigned. Little did I know at the time that there were differences in how inmates arrived, and that those differences were not lost on the general population of the prison. The "type" of uniform one arrived in made a clear statement, with no words ever being spoken. Some women arrive wearing orange, others wearing brown. This directly influenced the treatment they received from those within the facility. Entering the compound in the orange government-issued jumpsuit, referred to by the women as a "carrot suit," indicated the woman was *brought* to the prison by local law enforcement or federal marshals. Inherent in this observation was the idea that the woman did not come to prison *willingly*; she was strong-willed and determined. Brown-colored clothing meant the woman *gave in*, succumbed to the system—attached to this observation was the belief that she was weak.

The self-surrendered inmate draws curiosity from some, disdain from others. For some convicts it means nothing, as they are indifferent to most things in prison. For others, it sets up a clear target for intimidation, manipulation, and even violence. As a prisoner makes her way across the compound, one observes the standard "fresh fish" gaze. They ask questions about the woman and inquire whether she is new. For first timers such as myself, the chatter involves speculation. For those who have been incarcerated before, it becomes a "homecoming" ceremony of sorts. If returning convicts saw someone they knew (both guard and inmate), there was an exchange not unlike the welcome one receives from friends and family at the airport after a long trip. There was bantering and promises to get together after release from the orientation unit.

> As I walked across the compound it felt as if every eye in the place was on me. I felt ashamed and small. Watching the arrival of the shipments was something of a sport for many; I found it to be humiliating and pathetic. (journal entry)

I would later find myself participating in the observations about new prisoners despite my feelings about the practice.

Showing a lack of interest, or a departure from the warped display of group camaraderie, was seen as a weakness or an affront
to prisoner solidarity.

> The sound of a person walking in leg irons is unmistakable,
> strangely rhythmic and melodic. Maybe it's the paper
> shoes, a muffled rustling on the cement. How strange to see
> a woman hunched over in an ill-fitted carrot suit, hands
> and feet bound, faces that are empty and expressionless,
> following a guard clearly unconcerned as he walked quickly
> and without emotion. I hear the jingling of chains in my
> sleep, I wonder how long it will take me to get used to this
> world—to watching the arrival ceremony of new ship-
> ments, to the knot in my stomach that won't go away, to
> seeing myself the way others do as insignificant and worth-
> less. (journal entry)

Some women seemed unfazed and unaffected by their
return to prison. For some of the women, the shackled march
through the compound was actually taken lightly, almost
humorously. I did not understand these "homecoming" wel-
comes, perhaps because my pre-prison existence was not more
painful or more hopeless than what would be (or could be)
offered here. I could not comprehend how coming back to
prison could be cause for cheering and celebration.

It's Good Work if You Can Find It

> Walking around the compound, it's strange to hear some of
> the women address me as Ms. Olson—they know me from
> the Ed Center. Some have asked for help reading legal briefs
> and notes from their cases; some ask for help writing letters
> home. It made me feel a small amount of pride, but mostly
> it made me sad—a poignant reminder of who I was and
> what I used to do. Will I ever teach again? Will it (could it)
> ever be the same? Will I ever be the same? Do I *want* to be
> the same? (journal entry)

I got the job I had hoped for in the education department!
The facility here really does offer a lot to these women.
There are 3 basic levels of education, the ultimate goal of
taking and passing the GED, and a variety of programs like
cosmetology and business administration, as well as a com-
puter-focused business/tech type of program. The women

get pay increases for getting their GED or any other program completion or certificate. (letter to my brother)

I was lucky enough to land one of the coveted jobs as a "tutor" in the education center. There were a number of advantages to having such a job, including better pay (21 cents an hour as opposed to 11 to 20 cents an hour), better working conditions/hours, and sometimes deference from both convicts and staff. Having this job implied "education," and that garnered instant respect from most. When I first got the job, some of the women were angry because I had "jumped past" the initial job sequence (starting in the kitchen, moving into the laundry room, etc.). This did create friction and animosity.

The job also meant a certain amount of reverence (and tolerance) because now I had "access" to certain things—this was vital in the world of bartering, trading, and collecting. "Power" seemed to be attained in a variety of ways—the "skills" someone possessed (for example, being able to sew or alter clothing) or the ability to instill fear in others. I was able to "acquire" certain items during my stay, and this was significant to me, as well as some of the other women around me. Being able to "align" yourself with certain staff indeed had its benefits. As with most things in prison, there were times it also came with a heavy price.

> I've spent 2 months with the same fucking pair of socks—the ones I came in with! I was able to "acquire" more by swapping spiral notebooks with a gal who worked in the laundry room. At least the pair she stole for me were clean. I was able to provide some of the other women with various other "things"—this is also how I "came to possess" the extra blanket I used on my bunk. Had I gotten caught with it, I would have been sent to the hole for sure, but it was so worth it. You know me, I'm always cold, and sleeping with sweats and long johns on is clearly not enough for me. . . . Hiding it in my covers is tough, but there's a certain way to make your bunk, a jury-rigged short-sheet type of thing so the inspecting guards don't find the extra blanket. (letter to brother)

> I can't believe I am finally being sent to the camp that is close to my family. . . . I have heard they have similar jobs, plus, they also have a program whereby inmates train puppies, which are then placed through the PetSmart

stores. It sounds like one of the few opportunities where we might acquire a valuable skill (and much more enjoyable than driving a forklift). If nothing else, I would be able to train my next dog, which, in itself, is a real feat. (personal communication)

To its credit, FCI Tallahassee did offer a variety of programs geared towards self-awareness and personal improvement. Regardless of how a convict does time, there is always the underlying pressure to maintain a measure of dignity, an ounce of sanity, and most importantly, to survive. This takes a variety of forms and seems to influence every facet of prison culture.

I can't believe you wrote me a letter on the back of your "smoking cessation" certificate of completion!! (A) you don't smoke, and (B) I think we're going to frame it—Ha Ha. Why'd you take the class? Do they not care who signs up or why? Dennis thinks you took it because you're bored. I figure you took it because you're on some weird journey of self-improvement. Whatever the reason, it was definitely a fun letter. (letter from my brother)

I was used to teaching at the college level, but none of my educational experience prepared me for the types of women I'd meet, or the desperate and tragic needs they would display. To be fair, most of the time I hated this job! The women were "forced" to be there, which meant they made sure everyone around them was miserable too. The one main incentive to attend class was an increase in pay, but this motivated very few. Many of them signed up for the class as a way to get out of working. On more than one occasion, a woman would refuse to study, adamantly stating that she'd simply "buy" her GED when she got out. A number of the women, however, were more realistic in their frustration, wondering out loud why it would matter anyway when finishing their prison sentence meant going back to the same poor, destitute, disorganized neighborhood where job opportunities were limited, and education had little real meaning.

It was difficult for me to argue with the logic of the women as they discussed how education and training would impact their lives after release. It makes sense, on some level, that what we (FCI) teach them (whether math, science, masonry, or horticulture) will have only marginal influence on their abilities to find legitimate employment. It is good while they are "inside," as it fills the empty days and gives them something to do, but very little of what they learned would be practical in "their" world—they would not be returning to "my" world or the world of mainstream society. Their reality demands such very different things.

> My job here continues to go well . . . and I have been pro-moted so that I am now the Food Service clerk at the out-side warehouse, which means that I am essentially responsible for maintaining the paperwork and validating incoming shipments for the cafeteria and also for managing paperwork for all orders coming into the warehouse for office supplies, furniture, etc. The only thing I don't man-age paperwork for is the commissary and I am backup clerk for that portion of the responsibilities. While it is not the job I prefer, it is a pretty good job and uses some of my skillsets in office and problem management . . . plus, it keeps me busy which helps the time to pass faster. And faster is definitely a good thing! (personal communication)

One of the things I liked most about my job at the educa-tion center was that tutors had access to typewriters, which was useful for helping create classroom assignments for the women. The access also made it far easier to write letters to my friends and family. Working in the classroom was at times extremely difficult for me, although that had more to do with the unruly nature of the women and less to do with the mate-rial they were learning. The teacher with/for whom I worked was genuinely gifted. Not only did he "get" the women, but he also had an uncanny ability to elicit positive responses to the challenges he placed in front of them. He was one of the few people who could say anything to the women without any neg-ative consequences. The women did not always like him or agree with him, but they respected him. He didn't talk down to us, and he didn't seem to judge us. As long as we respected him, he was respectful of us. Given that we were both educators, I think in any other world, we could have been colleagues, and probably even friends. I looked forward to work, not just as a means of getting out of my unit for the day, but also because where I was working and for whom made me feel less like the convict I became and more like the professional I used to be.

> I like working with [_____] (teacher's name). He's friendly and funny. He talks to me like a human being, like

I might have something useful to contribute—like a peer. I
look forward to seeing him every day. (journal entry)

PRISON VIOLENCE

Research has found that physical violence is rare in
women's prisons (Kreager & Kruttschnitt, 2018). Verbal as well
as emotional aggression, however, are common. The general
absence of gangs in female institutions contributes to low levels
of physical aggression. Both men and women in prison have
histories of interpersonal violence, and victimization continues
to occur for many of these folks while they are in prison.
Rebecca Trammell, Timbre Wulf-Ludden, and Denise Mowder
(2015) used qualitative interviews with female inmates to
explore how the women themselves explain the fights and the
significance and effects of the altercations. The inmates inter-
viewed explained the informal social value of the fights—the
effects on networking in prison, the establishment of dominant
roles, and the nature of the relationships developed. This
research further suggests that the fights among the women
inmates are quite prevalent.

> Last week was a relatively bad week (although it's difficult
> to tell sometimes b/c so many things sucked . . .). Some
> woman beat the hell out of another gal in our unit while
> she was sleeping. The gal put a lock in a sock and took it to
> this gal's head. Stuff like that does happen fairly regularly,
> but not usually so close to home! Of course, an incident like
> that makes the rest of the unit edgy and tense. A lot of
> times I don't really get too bothered by the fights, but last
> week was one of the times where the physical threat of vio-
> lence and chaos, in combination with all the emotional stuff
> going on with the women on a personal level, gets so over-
> whelming. (letter to brother)

There are a multitude of media accounts describing prison
violence, often they highlight how severe and pervasive the
problems are, particularly with regards to men's prisons. Violence in prisons is typically a result of overcrowding, dismal
conditions, lack of officer/staff training (or being understaffed),
and abusive prisoner labor practices. One of the barriers to ade-
quately addressing prison violence is the belief that violence is a
normal and expected part of institutional life. Although there is

less overall violence in women's prisons, there are reports of female inmates being sexually abused by male officers (something I witnessed firsthand). These acts range from lewd remarks to forcible rape (see chapter 9).

Women can be mean and manipulative. It was not uncommon for a woman to provoke another inmate intentionally right before she was to be discharged. The antagonistic confrontation usually ended in a fight and a trip to the hole, thus delaying the release date. The situation played out a number of times while I was there. Depression, irritability, and the inability to ask for (and receive) help seemed to be the catalyst for many of the arguments among the women. Perhaps arguments were a subconscious way to create a diversion from the real issues with which we were dealing. Sometimes I think it's about survival, sometimes it's about entertainment, but most often it felt like hopelessness fueled by jealousy, frustration, and the realization that no one really gives a shit.

Many of the women are vulgar, violent, and hateful. It is difficult to know whether the women became this way by virtue of being locked up, or if they were equally as mean on the outside and subsequently imported the behavior into their prison life. It is probably a combination of both—a toxic environment aggravates and perpetuates destructive behavior. If a woman enters the facility physically and psychologically damaged, bitter, and vengeful, the prison culture does nothing to mitigate these conditions. It was genuinely difficult for me some days to feel sorry for or empathize with some of the women and their situations. While I generally hoped to provide help through my job at the education center and planned to advocate for prison reform after my release, there were times when I understand why society tends to view criminals with fear and contempt.

My perception of prison violence evolved during my incarceration. I initially equated the aggression displayed by the women to that of packs of wild animals—no discipline, no boundaries, no respect for others. When backed into a corner, they retaliate with aggression disproportionate to the situation at hand. Shamefully I viewed the women as society did— remorseless, cold, calculating, and deserving of the harsh punishment they receive. As time went on, I gradually started to see the women and interpret their behaviors with more understanding and compassion. It was largely because *my own* behavior changed. The shift was subtle, barely noticeable at first. Much like the other women, my temper grew short, and my usual turn-the-other-cheek personality was replaced with a volatility I did not recognize.

I remember lying on my bunk one night—amidst the cacophony of loud noises, the faint smell of burning food in the distance, and the seemingly endless clamoring of the metal bunks around me—thinking about a research project from the 1960s I had read about in school. The research focused on the effects of population density on behavior. As the number of rodents increased, the animals began to display a wide range of deviant behaviors, followed by such extreme psychological disruption that the animals eventually died off.

In that moment, I understood the herd mentality of the women. Influenced by the raw anxiety in each of us, we began to adopt (and engage in) certain behaviors on a largely emotional, rather than rational, basis. It began to make sense. Sadly, given the scarcity of resources in prison, nothing can be done *here* to fix or change this. In fact, most prison conditions exacerbate offender behavior. No rehabilitation takes place in the women who truly need it the most. This cruel environment amplifies the very same behaviors that it attempts to punish. Prisons were developed to decrease social disorder and violence. I would suggest that they have the opposite effect on inmates both inside the facility and in the communities to which the female prisoners return. The original goal of prisons as institutions of reform is completely undermined by the culture of fear and hostility that impacts every aspect of our prison experience.

> Did you hear about crazy [inmate name]? She's fucking crazy! She beat the shit out of [inmate name] with a hot iron because she jumped in front of her to iron her slacks! The bitch beat her within an inch of her life! Damn, that crazy [name] spends more goddamn time in the hole. (personal communication)

As I think back and examine the behavior of the women, the perpetual outbursts and outward demonstrations of aggression make sense—in me, as well as in the women around me. The almost childlike tantrums and complete meltdowns are symptoms of a struggle with emotions that are difficult to regulate. I was so often overwhelmed by frustration and fear that when confronted with an uncomfortable or painful situation, I reacted with aggression—much like the behavior I loathe in the other women. I felt an overall sense of injustice, triggering anxiety and overriding the logic that would typically enable me to see the situation with clarity. The explosive outpouring of feelings felt good in those moments.

> Today sucked! I got into it with B. again; she can be such a bitch. I know I am passive-aggressive, and that doesn't help the situation. Did I mention she's a bitch? A mean, rude, manipulative bitch. She's a hypocrite and that makes it even worse. She's got the Bible in one hand and the throat of another gal in the other. She demeans, provokes, incites, and I refuse to cower to her. Today was it; I'd had enough. I hate it when I can't control my anger. She and I seem to go through this about once a month. In addition to being a bitch; apparently she's a slow learner too! I should be bigger than this, I get that, but the "right" thing to do means different things in prison. It's not the same as being on the outs. She will be here long after I'm gone and that secretly makes me smile. . . . I hate that part of myself. (journal entry)

> It's like a fucking block party in here tonight—1:30 in the morning and I have yet to see a guard. There's so much noise, the yelling, the swearing, the fighting, the sex, the grocery store next-door (some gal's locker) reeks . . . if society saw this, they'd probably call for even more severe sentencing, and tonight, I just might agree with them. (journal entry)

THE PROTEST(S)

Riots are a part of prison history. Prior to the 1960s, most riots were unplanned, uncoordinated protests over prison conditions; they were *frustrations riots* (Shelden et al., 2016).

> In the prison environment, prisoners have few options to improve the conditions under which they live. Occupying a position of powerlessness removes most possibilities for negotiation. Frustration and rage sometimes boil over into violence, protests, and riots. (p. 294)

Prison populations changed during the 1960s with an influx of more educated and politically sophisticated young whites and African Americans convicted of drug-law violations and protest activities. Militant inmates believed they were part of an oppressed class, and a growing number of prisoners extended protests beyond prison conditions to protests over the prison as an aspect of economic and political oppression. The result was *political riot*. One of the most violent took place at Attica in 1971 after the killing of George Jackson, field marshal of the Black Panthers Party, at San Quentin for allegedly trying to escape on August 21, 1971. On September 9, more than half the men incarcerated at Attica took 38 prison guards hostage and forced negotiations for 4 days. The governor of New York ordered the state police to attack; 10 hostages and 29 inmates were killed. The riot attracted widespread media attention, and the unity of the prisoners prompted a nationwide prison reform movement.

The peak number of riots was in 1973. By 2003, riots were rare despite exponential growth in the prison population (Shelden et al., 2016). Once again, changing prison demographics contributed to the reduced number of prison riots. Nonviolent offenders comprised a higher percentage of the prison population. In addition, the proliferation of super-maximum-security prisons removed the more violent prisoners from the general population. Another factor has been court intervention in some systems that mandated improved living conditions.

While riots are a rare part of prison life, they still occur. Some riots are spontaneous, while others, similar to the one that took place when I was at FCI, are planned out in advance. Crowded conditions, bad food, lack of medical services, and poor plumbing, heating, lighting, and ventilation create stress for inmates that can lead to riots.

In fall 2016, prisoners across the country engaged in a number of sit-ins, silent protests, and outright violent outbursts in an attempt to bring attention to prison conditions. The prisoners organized strikes in what was thought to be the largest prison strike in United States history. On September 6, 2016, over 46 facilities experienced work strikes, preemptive shutdowns, hunger strikes, or some other form of disruption. An estimated 57,000 prisoners participated or were locked down to prevent their participation (Incarcerated Workers, 2018).

With the help of friends, family, and outside prisoner support groups, inmates organized and carried out demonstrations over poor prison conditions and prison labor practices characterized as modern-day slavery. In all, there were protests in 17 states in variety of facilities. The little-known protests were organized around September 9th in commemoration of the 45th anniversary of the bloody revolt at the Attica Correctional Facility in New York.

Budget cuts, hiring freezes, or inadequate administration of personnel can lead to lack of basic services for inmates, improper supervision, and poor security. This creates tension among inmates and between inmates and staff that can lead to riots. Public apathy and a "get tough" attitude toward prisoners, creates a focus on incapacitation and less emphasis on treatment and programming. As inmates internalize being ostracized from society, they can become alienated, leading to riots.

> Big news today, they confiscated all of the typewriter cartridges on the compound, even the ones at school that I type my personal letters on. A coup was being planned (poor medical treatment, price gouging in the commissary, and the reigning queen of terror herself—Lt ___). Someone typed up flyers, made several hundred copies and tried to distribute them around the prison. The Lt saw a bunch of the flyers posted up in the dog unit's (unit D) laundry room and she had a fit! That's when all hell broke loose. They ran the typewriter cartridges through some machine at the SIS office (internal affairs), I'm not completely certain if that is how they found out who started this. My bunkie was questioned this morning. Not only does she work with the gal who got caught (in the electronics department), but apparently she received a shot, was shipped out of here, and sequestered for 8 months—her charge at the time was "inciting a riot." She had been part of a group that "acted together" 8 or 10 years ago for better dining hall/food services. Because she was part of that, they automatically assumed she was part of this—once a convict always a convict. At this point, 3 women have been sent to the hole. (letter to my brother)

During my time at FCI Tallahassee, I experienced several instances of prisoner group-resistance. Most were not riots in the truest sense, however. I was privy to the planning of a/the major revolt, and I did intend to participate. In the midst of the nonstop cattiness among the women, it was refreshing to witness the way they organized and rallied in support of one another to demand better food, medical care, and improved treatment by the guards. Prison officials knew a bit about what the women were planning. The warden, office personnel, thera-

peutic staff, teachers, and additional guards were all on hand
supervising the compound that night. What they did not know
was that the demonstration was meant to be a silent protest.
We would not have been out in the compound; we would have
been inside our units staging a peaceful "sit-in."

> You know something's going down tonight, look, they got
> the teachers wandering the compound, and even the shrink
> from medical is standing over there talking to *Miami Vice* (a
> derogatory term for one of the lieutenants). (personal com-
> munication)

The facility-wide attempt at a coup ultimately resulted in
86 women being shipped out of the facility for their involvement. It was never really clear to us how the authorities determined who was and who was not a part of the protest planning.
As we were routinely told, "our understanding was not important." As the events unfolded, the unity crumbled. It was dis-
heartening to witness the complete collapse of the prisoner
camaraderie. The initial solidarity quickly disappeared as the
women began to turn on each other. Vendettas were "evened
up," and because it doesn't take much to set a fellow prisoner up
on false accusations, a number of the women lied to the authorities in attempt to get others punished. The prison's response
was to put us on 24-hour lockdown; this was far more painful
than a trip to the hole. After several days of being in cramped
quarters with 240 volatile and angry women, I would have rel-
ished the silence of solitary confinement. Throughout the lockdown, officers would randomly pull women from the cubicles,
taking them away to be interrogated. Some would be returned
back to their bunks; others were not seen again.

> You should have seen the sight, all these women handcuffed
> and marched through the compound . . . they're locking
> people up first and asking questions later. Now I'm starting
> to get a little scared about the roundup of the inmates.
> Today was the second day and as far as I know, there will
> be another round tomorrow. I've got no involvement, but
> that doesn't seem to matter! They've taken 2 of the
> "tutors," a number of women from the law library, and a
> few others from the school [education center]. I'm scared
> because the BOP officials are going on the words of other
> inmates, and you know women are naming names simply
> to help themselves. It's perfectly acceptable to shackle a gal

and ship her off to Miami—guilty by association has a whole new meaning around here. Sure I've pissed off my fair share of people (guard and convict), and Lord knows I've made outright complaints and accusations in letters and on the phone, but nothing like what they are describing—things that were on the flyers (statutes, codes, inmate rights, etc.). (letter to my brother)

There's been talk of us taking on the prison for the shitty way they treat us, not talking violence or anything, mainly just refusing to work our jobs, refusing to go to the dining hall and more or less just refusing to do anything the pigs want us to. Even though I'm glad you're out, I still wish you were here, we could have some fun. (personal communication)

Chapter Six

Doing Time

There is a long history of research on the culture of men's prisons, while experiences of incarcerated women were long ignored. Society ascribed a lesser status to women, viewing them as less powerful than men; those characteristics carried over to life in prison (Stohr, Jonson, & Lux, 2015). In addition, the number of imprisoned women is substantially lower than the number of imprisoned men, contributing to women prisoners being viewed historically as less worthy of attention. Female prisoners serve time in correctional systems designed for and frequently operated by men. Incarcerated women were a forgotten population; their specific needs and issues were ignored. Like men, women suffer the same pains of imprisonment identified for men more than 50 years ago—loss of liberty, autonomy, goods and services, heterosexual relationships, and security. Their methods for adapting to the deprivations differ.

> I've been doing time for 20 years off and on. For me it's like being detained from my life. Everything is put on hold, except I continue to get old. I've really wasted half of my life in prison, but it's the price we pay, right? (personal communication)

In the late 1990s, scholars began documenting the conditions of confinement for women and their modes of adaptation (Kreager & Kruttschnitt, 2018). Barbara Owen (1998) conducted ethnographic research on how women learn to do prison and the factors that affect how women in institutions organize their time and create a social world. Just as there are different patterns in the offenses committed by men and women, there are also differences in the social organization of prison lives.

Women's prison culture is linked to gender role expectations of sexuality and family. Owen found support for the importation model (pre-prison experiences dictate how inmates negotiate and live through imprisonment) of prison culture as well as the indigenous (deprivation) model (the pains of imprisonment are the primary influences on responses to incarceration). The size of the prison and its population influence the daily lives of inmates. Race and ethnic identities provide a subtext, but they are secondary to the dominant issue of personal relationships in women's prisons.

Most convicts will tell you that you can do your time, or the time will do you. Some inmates do easier time than others because they adopt the customs and culture that exists within prison. For them, prison becomes their life. They immerse themselves in the lives of those around them.

> I believe doing time is what you bring to it. If you bring a positive attitude to the situation, then the "time" can be something productive in your life. In my situation, I did not get a lot of time. If I'd been sentenced to 15 or 20 or 30 years, I may have a completely different attitude about doing my time. (personal communication)

They fully participate in pseudofamilies and homosexual relationships that provide affection, comfort, and support. Individuals who are sentenced to prison must learn to adapt to the caged world around them (Owen, 1998). Other convicts steer clear of the relationship aspects of prison, choosing instead to focus on improving themselves. This could be done through a variety of programming (i.e., earning a GED), vocational training, or simply making use of the library and the reading/research material available.

Racial identity is not a significant factor in the social structure of women's prisons (Kreager & Kruttschnitt, 2018). It has little influence on who is politically active, but it sometimes surfaces for white women unaccustomed to being a minority. Age is an important element in understanding women's prison experiences. Prison for a young woman who has never been imprisoned before can be isolating and frightening. Older women can be a stabilizing presence in prison. As the age structure of the prison population changes, more attention has focused on older inmates. Between 2008 and 2012, the number of women sentenced to life in prison increased 14%. The number of female prisoners aged 55 or older quadrupled from 1993 to 2013. In 2017, almost 8% of women prisoners were 55 or older (Bronson & Carson, 2019). Changes in penal practices affect the experiences of women prisoners. Societal views that emphasize punishment and coercive control affect the attitudes of prison employees and result in weakened inmate-staff trust and inmates retreating from the institution and one another.

Women often construct social worlds with various rules within the prison. One prison subculture is known as "the mix." Women in this subculture are involved in drugs, fights with other prisoners, engaging in gossip, and generalized conflict (Owen et al., 2017). Some women spend their time alone and in silence, separate and away from virtually all aspects of communal prison life. Still others fill their time with violence and rule violating. The quotation that follows is from a 27-year-old FCI inmate who was 9 years into a life sentence for a nonviolent drug offense.

> When I first got here I didn't care about anything. I let myself go. I cried all the time. I kept to myself. It was lonely and it made the days long and the nights even longer. A couple of years into my sentence I decided that it wouldn't beat me. The system took my freedom, the state took my kids, and I was here for life. But they can't take what's here [pointing to her chest and her head] unless you let them. The bastards don't get my soul. I get up every morning, fix my hair and do my make-up. I get pedicures on the weekends, and I help others with their hair and their fashion . . . it makes me feel useful, like I have meaning. I've made friends here; I have a girlfriend who cares about me. This is my life now, it's no longer painful, I've accepted it and I've adjusted. I gave up hope a long time ago. (personal communication)

We had a certain amount of latitude in what we did with our free time. Some would stay in their bunks and read; others would steal away to the iron pile for intimate relations; still others simply sat outside talking with others or reading by themselves. It bothered me the first time I noticed women laughing and seemingly enjoying their time together. I wondered how it was possible to have fun in such a miserable place. It was offensive that they could smile and socialize, waving at each other across the compound as if at a mall or a park in the city. I didn't understand how they could be happy here. Then one day, while walking back from the education center where I worked, I heard my name hollered from across the compound. There stood several of my friends, talking loudly and motioning for me to come join them. At that moment, I realized I had become like those women I despised earlier. What I found was that it was not about forgetting where we were, or about mocking the system that had put us here—it was about feeling human and wanted and valued. It was about finding safety and security in a world where those things are carefully manufactured and easily destroyed.

> How the fuck are you dude? Are you ok? I heard that fucking [inmate] went off and tore up the fucking classroom. . . . With the police cracking down on all this riot shit, they're sending people to the hole first and asking questions later. We were worried about you [reaching out to hug me]. (personal communication)

> I've been having bunkie woes—what the fuck is wrong with these women? Mrs. [inmate name] went to the SHU for practicing voodoo out in the yard. Apparently she owed someone money and thought she'd rather curse her then pay her. Then, [inmate name] left (you remember her, right?), and [inmate name] moved in. She was a practicing Muslim, on her knees five times a day praying . . . she then gets a 205 on the iron pile. [A 205 refers to a disciplinary write-up for sexual contact.] Now I've got [inmate name], I like her, and it's working much better. (personal communication)

WHAT TO DO TODAY

Socializing was a large part of the evening routine. I was initially perplexed by the time, effort, and energy that the women put into "fixing" themselves up to simply go outside on the compound. Elaborate hairdos and over-the-top makeup were not uncommon. On some evenings, it looked as if the women were going "clubbing" in the real world. Clothing would be ironed, and perfume would be sprayed. I must admit, however, that I was caught off guard the first time I encountered an incredibly masculine looking woman—in fact, the first night I ventured out to the compound, I was certain it was a co-ed facility. Watching the women take part in these very fundamental "dating" rituals fascinated me. Some of the women casually interacted with one another, while others were clearly going outside to meet their "significant other." Initially it seemed like such as waste, going through all the primping and the posturing. Later I realized it served the same purpose as the camaraderie I originally loathed. We may be caged like animals, but we are human, we have intellect, we have feelings, we have needs, we have lives that deserve to be lived. Here is where it seemed to matter the most.

> I've been getting some body art these last couple of months. Three new tats! 2 crosses; Celtic and biker crosses on the back of both arms above the elbow. Something like that (an arrow pointing to a picture drawn in the letter), but better! The other one is a red and black nautical star behind my right ear. Damn sweet, too! We're thinking about another one on the other side in a different color. I've got plans to get more, like my hubby's name. I've thought about a barbed wire arm band like yours, maybe I'll do that too. They're so addictive. It's better to do them in the winter when I can cover them with long sleeves. I'll see if I can muster up some pics for you. It's fucked up, but you know society loathes the tatt'd convict; little do they realize we're just normal people. (personal communication)

I spent much of my time writing and reading—as much material as I could get. My family, as well as the few friends I managed to keep throughout the process, often sent me books and articles to read. Keeping occupied was crucial for me; I found that when I was bored, I had the tendency to fall into the drama of the women around me.

> Thank you for the book you sent. I also received a letter and an article from one of the convict crim guys. I read the article several times, I'm not sure whether it's the shared story and validation, or the fact that I actually miss reading academic-type material, either way, it was good to have. (letter to my brother)

The majority of what I read covered specific criminal justice topics—for example, I read *Convict Criminology*, a book with firsthand accounts of ex-convicts who were convicted of a crime, served time, and became university scholars. This book gave me hope! Some of the women would give me odd looks when they noticed what I was reading, others were interested in the topics and requested to read the material when I had finished. On occasion one of the guards would say something derogatory (of course) about "criminals being too stupid for college," but on balance, they were not too concerned with my prison-related readings. One day during count, my case manager walked by my bunk and picked up the book I was reading at the time (Austin and Irwin's *It's About Time: America's Imprisonment Binge*). She was not the least bit surprised as she was aware of my background and education; however, she did not seem pleased.

Waiting for daily mail call and planning visitations with friends consumed me. My brother lived in Seattle, too far way for visits, but he wrote me often. I eagerly looked forward to his letters and the times I was able to call him. I was not the only inmate focused on getting mail. For many of us, it was the best part of each and every day. There were a number of women who never received mail and/or had no one to talk to on the phone. I cannot imagine how lonely that would feel—I remember thinking how sad that some of these women did not exist to anyone outside the prison.

> Hey Bubba, you'll have to forgive the handwriting in this letter, it's still fairly dark out (I get some light from a nearby window) and they haven't turned on the lights yet. It's Monday morning and I'm so excited to see Julie and the boys that I got up early. . . . I actually didn't plan it this way; I obviously don't sleep well here. For once it's quiet, and it gave me some much-needed privacy with my hygiene routine. I fixed a big cup of coffee, made my bunk, and figured I'd write you a letter. (letter to my brother)

I also learned to crochet while I was in prison, and it is still something I do today. In the commissary I was able to purchase yarn, needles, and even a variety of other craft-related items. My grandmother spent years crocheting and knitting. She encouraged me to take up the hobby, but I never seemed to have the time. She would have loved the fact that I finally learned the family trade—although I'm sure the fact that I didn't acquire the skill until I was in prison would have made her *far less* happy.

There is a lot of truth to the old adage about prisoners learning to be better criminals while they are in prison. In addition to some of the new "pro-social" behaviors I learned (i.e., crocheting), I did pick up a few that could definitely have made me a smarter, harder-to-catch convict. One of the 3 women I spent most of my time with was serving a 7-year sentence for making and disseminating bombs. I liked her immensely—despite her penchant for bomb making. She was warm, and funny, and incredibly smart. She had an awkwardness to her that made her likable and endearing. I left prison knowing how to make a number of incendiary devices—from a Molotov cocktail, to a gas-tank bomb, to an exploding portable brazier. I would clearly never use any of this knowledge, but prison afforded me the opportunity to learn criminal behavior.

The deprivations of prison taught us to be resourceful in many of our day-to-day activities. I had the same 2 pairs of socks for almost my entire prison stay; they were not particularly thick or well-made, so I wore holes in them regularly. When I could not purchase sewing materials in the commissary, I used dental floss to darn the holes. I learned that dental floss is not only a sturdy material, but it can be used for a number of prison repair projects. Some of my days were spent making lipstick and blush out of red markers, learning to make prison wine from fruit cocktail, sugar, and bread, and microwaving ice cream and Little Debbie chocolate rolls to make fudge. I hoarded sanitary napkins from the education center not only for their traditional use but also because we were required to clean our lockers, bunks, and cubicles. Mops, buckets, and other cleaning appliances were not always available (which didn't seem to matter to the inspecting officers). I discovered that maxi-pads make perfect mop heads and washing rags. They were also great at lining the windows that leaked in rainstorms! Idle time was difficult, but we did manage to fill our days with a variety of nondestructive activities.

> Today I learned to light a cigarette with a battery and a razor blade—no shit! Its easier to do with tin foil or a paperclip, but this is prison, so nothing's easy, right? (letter to my brother)

> I'm so bored today. I've written 3 letters so far. I have yet to be called for work this morning—it's another one of our fog days. I'm from Texas, I had no idea it got so foggy here in the wintertime. You know how we go into lock-down on times like this; they're so afraid someone might escape. God forbid the dude running the perimeter checks might finally get to put one in the chamber and shoot someone! (personal communication)

Prison as Opportunity

Spending the majority of my time in the education center, I noticed that a significant number of the women were surprisingly appreciative of the programs and opportunities available to them while incarcerated. A common theme was that prison was offering them respite from their chaotic, cruel, and harsh pre-prison lives. For some, prison was indeed a better place.

> For so many of the women here, this is the best they've ever had it. This is home . . . and for the first time in their lives, they have regular meals, a job, a schedule and a routine, and at least marginal medical/dental services. I've talked to women who have never been to a library before coming here. I see women who labor for long periods to press their khakis (and even their grays), and I suspect they never had ready access to an iron in their childhoods. This place allows many women to totally break away from the responsibilities of the world (motherhood, etc.) for a little while. With the right marketing plan, some could even sell this as a resort for those wanting to really escape!! But even if that were true, I think it reflects poorly on our society. What kind of society allows prison to be better than neighborhoods and communities in the free world? (journal entry)

Despite the pains of deprivation, prison served as a much-needed "intervention" for some. These women were surprisingly positive and constructive about the time they were serving. They were able to recognize that something was wrong in their lives and that changes needed to be made. Their drug and alcohol addictions had clouded their minds and devastated their lives.

> I don't hate prison. I love prison and think anybody who has experienced the lifestyle that I've lived . . . the drugs, the selling drugs, running from the police daily, staying up all night for days, never at peace. (personal communication)

There were a few women who viewed prison as an opportunity to pay attention to the things they didn't when they were outside the walls. Some of these women viewed prison as a way station in their cycle of drug use, prostitution, and street crime.

> For me, doing this time is like a hiatus from the hustle and bustle of my hectic life. It is a "time out" for me to stop and think about the direction of my life. Of course, I would not

have willingly chosen prison as a get-away vacation, but now that I am here, it's not anything I imagined it to be. (personal communication)

Unfortunately, a significant number of women, despite the positive self-reflections and the desire to do right after release, will never get the opportunity to right their wrongs. They are serving lengthy sentences and parole no longer exists in the federal system. Draconian sentencing policies eliminate second chances for many inmates. Many in society support long, mandatory sentences—with a notable lack of concern for countless hours of idle time. There are calls for eliminating the expense of athletic equipment, entertainment such as televisions or playing cards, and educational enhancements such as books or computers. Opportunities for self-improvement are lost and hopes for a better life on the outside are dashed.

Staring across the compound I am overcome with feelings of sadness at the day that awaits me. Our daily lives are both ominous and painful. Our days reek of hopelessness and shame. There is a repetition in everything we do—work, conversation, interactions—it all seems so meaningless. This *is* as painful as it is supposed to be, but what of restoration and healing? We are caged and warehoused, discarded as human refuse. (journal entry)

The new warden is making some huge changes and emphasizes control of movement. This means no more evenings spent outside or at the track. It means basically being locked down 24 hours a day. You know all this is going to do is bring the chaos and violence from outside into the units. . . . What do they suppose that is going to do to us? I guess they really don't care, huh? (personal communication)

WHAT'S FOR DINNER?

It is worth noting the extraordinary amount of "commerce" in the prison. The government feeds, clothes, and houses us—but amenities are scarce. A minimalistic life is part of the punishment, and everyone from correctional administrators, guards, and staff emphasized this point. One reason was to maintain compliance and security. On another level, some of the staff wanted to remind us continually that we were being punished! I noticed, however, that any emphasis on making us miserable seemed to have the exact opposite effect. Sure, we were unhappy, but deprivation prompted interesting forms of ingenuity and entrepreneurship.

Certain positions within the prison, for example, provided some of the women with a variety of opportunities for independent "initiatives." I witnessed women stealing from administrative offices, work sites, educational classrooms, the psychological testing and therapy offices, and especially the kitchen and laundry areas—nothing was off-limits from the thievery (except maybe the chapel). Depending on your job assignment, women had the ability to steal food, clothing, building materials, and even information to sell or trade to other women. It was truly amazing to watch these systems of trade and commerce.

> I'm sorry I haven't written in awhile, I've been sort-of caught up in all the garbage that's been going on here—as of March 1st this will be a smoke-free environment. They ran out of cigarettes at the commissary 3 weeks ago. It is very sad what is taking place in here. People are trading for smokes at extremely high prices. One cigarette goes for $2 to $5, and a pack for $20 to $85. People are trading hygienes, stamps and coffee, and it's very sad how others (nonsmokers) are taking advantage of the situation. (personal communication)

The kitchen and the dining hall were popular places to steal things. Reusable, sealable storage bags were one of the most valuable commodities to have; one could store coffee, rice, sugar, or pills in them. Kitchen workers, on some level, were able to regulate what was brought into the units and parceled out to the women. Deprivation of the most basic belongings made these exchanges powerful. Various commodities could be bought and sold, and the simplest things appeared to hold the most value. I was surprised, and actually impressed, with the number of women who rarely ate in the dining hall; they didn't need too. They would make some of the most amazing meals with minimal ingredients.

Lockers often took on the look of grocery stores. Unfortunately, it was not uncommon to smell rotten meat or spoiled vegetables coming from certain areas. I remember listening to the women tell about how certain items were taken from the dining hall. For example, some of the women would steal chunks of meat or game hens (a special treat for our holiday meals). This process started by placing the food in plastic bags, and then putting them in the dumpster to be picked up later. It was all very well thought out and very well choreographed. We were subjected to regular shakedowns by the guards. Depending on who was in charge, the consequences could be severe. Most women seemed undeterred by this threat of punishment.

MERCY IN THE CHAPEL

Because the First Amendment guarantees the "free exercise" of religion, religious programs are available to everyone in prison. In the past, religious programs have always been a mainstay of prison services but were regarded as an offshoot of prison life rather than a treatment program (Clear et al., 2019). Some scholars and activists view religion as a means of helping people change their lives. Florida, Iowa, Kansas, Minnesota, and Texas have opened prison treatment facilities with a central philosophy of religious teaching. Religion helps prisoners by providing a "psychological and physical 'safe haven' from harsh realities and enables people to maintain ties with their families and with religious volunteers from the outside" (p. 365) Many administrators attribute a more stabilized prison culture to strong religious groups, which makes running the prison easier. Participation in religious programs helps prisoners adjust to prison and reduces disciplinary infractions.

> Having done just under 5 years, I finally feel like I needed this time to get to know myself and to find out the true purpose for my life. I feel like God has given me a second chance. (personal communication)

The music at the chapel was extraordinary, capable of lifting spirits of listeners through feelings of being transported elsewhere. I am not a fan of the traditional hymns typically heard in church, but the FCI choir was like nothing I had ever heard before (or probably will ever again). It was made up of some of the most talented and gifted women I have ever encountered. Their voices were amazing and could produce goose bumps on even the most hard-core criminal. There was a passion in their singing not seen elsewhere, it was incredibly uplifting and infectious, and it made the most painful of situations tolerable (if only for just a few minutes).

I was brought up Catholic, but my spirituality has waxed and waned over the years. While I do believe in some sort of "higher power" (whatever that might be), I don't seek strength or search for comfort in that belief. However, I was truly fascinated by the faith that was displayed around me and was drawn to the women's ability to believe in something so fervently. The religious community of the prison was as varied as the women themselves. The chapel welcomed a number of religious groups; there were services for Catholics, Muslims, Confucians, and Wiccans. The pastoral leaders demonstrated great compassion and understanding to all of us—a true rarity in the hellish prison existence.

You cannot be a convict in prison without hearing the old joke that "God must live in prison, because that seems to be where most people find him." It makes me cringe to look back on my time there and think about how cruel and offensive that statement is. Certainly, there are those who use misuse or misrepresent their association with all things spiritual as a "tool"—perhaps to do better at a parole hearing, or to curry favors with prison staff, or to present a false veneer of remorse for crimes committed. Much to my surprise, many of the women went to the chapel for themselves—for healing, for guidance, and for forgiveness.

I was sitting with a group of women one afternoon following the death of one of the inmates, when, as often happens, the conversation went to "seeing the good in a bad situation." The women offered up personal stories of strength and survival through faith—and how one can't have light without dark, good without evil, and the like. I could see that they wore these stories of healing and forgiveness like a warm blanket. On some level I was jealous at the peace they seemed to have found and the anger they had let go. I was able to find solace in the chapel, but for me it was less about "finding religion," and more about the women and the comfort I found in their presence. It seemed to be one of the few places where judgments and crimes were cast aside, a place where we interacted as women, plain and simple. We were all children of *some* God (whether it be Allah or Muhammad or whomever), and therefore we were all redeemable.

I admired the religious devotion and enthusiasm displayed by many of the women. Some of them would spend inordinate amounts of time cutting up scriptures from booklets and various other sources, folding them up, and passing out the messages to us as we walked through the compound in the mornings. Despite my lack of spiritual direction, I was welcomed into these groups, my questions of doubt and skepticism were met with understanding and, at times, laughter. Perhaps it was their tolerance that drew me to them—tolerance of the pain and suffering around us, tolerance of having a nonbeliever in their midst, tolerance of the system that clearly lacks justice and equality, tolerance for all the things we cannot change. I longed for my own warm blanket of forgiveness and, perhaps, relief from looking for it everywhere but from within.

In addition to regular church services, the chapel and its ministers provided a variety of study groups, choir groups, and sing-a-longs, plus one-on-one spiritual guidance. The services themselves were an odd combination of scripture, sermon, sharing, prayer, and music. I looked forward to the Sunday services. The messages of the sermon were decidedly relevant, as the pastor(s) addressed personal and emotional issues significant to incarcerated women. Chapel services offered one of the very few places where we could go and simply "be." At the services, we were not the sum of our crimes; we were not defined by our offenses; rather, we were women who had lost our way in life. We had made mistakes, but behavior was separated from the person in the chapel. The messages were often about redemption and mercy, both to ourselves and to those we'd hurt. The various chaplains I met seemed to be especially aware of the special needs of the female inmates. They did not make excuses for or condone what we had done, but they offered prayers of hope and compassion.

> We want each of you to show the same diligence to the very end, so that what you hope for may be realized in the end. (Hebrews 6:11) [One of the slips of paper cut and distributed in the morning by some of the women on the compound.]

Chapter Seven

The Humanity We Deserve

Every single being, even those who are hostile to us, is just as afraid of suffering as we are, and seeks happiness in the same way we do. Every person has the same right as we do to be happy and not suffer. So let's take care of others wholeheartedly, of both our friends and our enemies. This is the basis for true compassion.
—The Dalai Lama XIV

Critical social problems such as sexual abuse, substance abuse, mental illness, family fragmentation, economic instability, and social isolation have particularly impacted women in the criminal justice system. These women often lack adequate health care services, mental health assistance, quality educations, and employment opportunities that are largely associated with reduced criminal behavior. If criminogenic conditions had been addressed prior to incarceration, the women I met could have become law-abiding and productive citizens.

Unfortunately, society seems to pay little attention to the plight of many of these marginalized women until they break the law. Sadly, we have criminalized poverty and mental illness to the point that our nation's prisons and jails are filled with those folks least able to pay fines, seek medical attention, and secure adequate housing and employment. Legislators, the public, and justice officials are then shocked when recidivism rates are high, and the women don't seem to have "learned their lessons." Women receive no help addressing and overcoming the conditions that precipitated their initial contact with the justice system. It seems absurd to assume that a stint in prison will change the preexisting conditions in an offender's life—and even more ridiculous that it will change their lives after release. The criminal justice system is not designed to deal with many of the conditions in which crime breeds.

Incarcerated women have high levels of drug addiction and dependency, as well as long histories of violence and trauma. Prior to incarceration, many women live lives on the fringes of society—homeless and struggling with poverty and cycles of victimization. Childhood trauma, especially for women, puts them at significant risk for future involvement in the justice system. Anecdotal evidence from the women I met strongly suggests that formative childhood experiences of violence and abuse result in mental health issues, multiple suicide attempts, alcohol and drug abuse, and eating disorders. Yet despite these needs, services and programming for women in the justice system are decidedly inadequate, especially gender-specific services designed to address the realities of these women effectively (Krisberg, Marchionna, & Hartney, 2015).

The high rate of recidivism among young women, many of whom are sole supporters of children, is an important indicator of problems with current correctional practices. Many female offenders return to the streets facing the same issues they faced prior to sentencing. While research on women and girls continues to grow, the reality is that we still know very little about women's pathways to crime, as well as how best to assist and treat them once they are locked up. It is admittedly difficult for correctional administrators to manage a population they seem to know so little about.

> So far the new warden has been making some minor changes. For instance, we no longer get to walk up the main sidewalk. Staff only! Seems to many "officials" that us lowly inmates weren't yielding to the cowardly cops! No sleeves up at rec either, and a whole bunch of other petty shit. She's a bit of a clean freak, always obsessing about the conditions of everyone's floors. But on a good note, it seems like she's not bringing in as many new inmates, which is great. You know how overcrowded this place has been. Our count (which I get at work) is 1077 women, 216 men. Our usual count is 1260 and 300. I hear she's trying to drop count so she can close A and D units for repairs. We'll see if that happens, but whatever the case—it's alright with me. (personal communication)

The dramatic rise in the women's prison population is the result of shifts in the criminal justice system's response to female offending. The war on drugs resulted in legislation that mandated prison terms for possession of illicit substances—a shortsighted, punitive response. Minor property offenses also account for a significant proportion of female incarceration. Instead of a policy of last resort, imprisonment has become the first order response for a wide range of women offenders, including those swept up in the war on drugs. The "zero-tolerance" approach to drugs also resulted in obstacles to reentry through banning access to public housing for drug offenses.

Punitive policies overlook the fiscal and social costs of imprisonment. Further, cuts to crucial social services, educational programs, and other barriers to economic success eliminate opportunities to prevent female offending. The money used to fund and perpetuate correctional budgets could be spent far more wisely on areas that would improve rather than dilute social capital. Most female offenders lack positive community relationships and social networks, employment-relevant knowledge and skills, and legitimate work experiences that could insulate them from criminality. "Improving the social and human capital of women offenders improves their chances of desisting from criminal behavior in the community" (Owen et al., 2017, p. 10).

In my 6 months as FCI Tallahassee, I met hundreds of women, the majority of whom were nonviolent drug-offenders. I did meet a woman serving 7 years for child molestation, child rape, and crimes stemming from the acts and solicitation of these crimes on the Internet. Far more frequently, I spent times with women serving 20+ years to life for illegal drug crimes ranging from possession, use, and conspiracy (a judicially flexible charge). FCI Tallahassee, like most facilities, warehouses far more drug offenders for longer periods of time than those charged with violent crimes. In the federal system, more than half of female federal prisoners were serving a sentence for drug trafficking (Bronson & Carson, 2019).

The following statements from women at FCI Tallahassee highlight the punitive nature of this country's drug laws.

> I got caught up in the federal conspiracy laws, and you know this gives out sentences that don't match our crimes. I'm the first to admit I sold drugs for almost 10 years, but

it was to support myself and my family. We were poor. Not really an excuse, I know, but my mom sold me to a man to support her drug habit. He was almost 40 and I was 14. He gave me love and attention and cared for me. But then he threw me away. Because of him, I'm here doing 20 years. (personal communication)

I am 27 years old. I've never been in trouble. I'm a first-time offender, my crime was not violent. My original sentence was life plus 5 years for conspiracy. In 1996, my sentence was reduced to 35 years, but in 1997 this sentence was vacated, and in 1998, I was resentenced to 85 years. (personal communication)

It is estimated that 80-85% of women in prison are incarcerated for crimes that directly result from their relationships with an abusive partner. (Law, 2019) Many of these women had no previous contact with the legal system; for the most part, they pose very low levels of risk to community safety. Women typically get into trouble with the law for very different reasons than do men. The research on women's criminal histories supports what I saw in the female prisoners around me—motivations to commit crime often had to do with survival, providing for their children, coping with early trauma, and unhealthy relationships with partners who would be considered chronic offenders.

SECURITY

If they were not yelling at us or writing us up for random and inane rule infractions, most guards walked past us as if we were invisible. They simply tuned us out, their expressions blank or cynical. I suppose they were weary, believing they had seen and heard it all. Perhaps too often they had heard the women complain, deny responsibility, or project blame onto others for their own misbehaviors. Perhaps it made their job easier, seeing us as only as numbers, statistics, or trash. Many of the women I met had undoubtedly been treated as second-class citizens most of their lives. Why should this place be any different?

Why must they yell at us? Why are they so angry? Why do they fight over everything? Grown women fighting and acting out as they struggle to have some small amount of control. I'm not sure who's more pitiful—the women or the guards. (personal communication)

It would be unfair to categorize all guards or prison staff as evil. There were indeed those few who didn't think it was necessary to yell at us constantly or to talk down to us. There were a few who actually talked *with* us. Some would ask about family members, the current status of court cases, or health issues; occasionally, they would even share humor, jokes, and laughter. Unfortunately, these individuals were few and far between. Some officers and prison staff could recognize when discipline was necessary and when a friendlier, relaxed approach was appropriate. The women responded to this balanced approach with respect and a willingness to accept direction. Referent power in a penal institution refers to compliance gained through an inmate's respect for an officer (Wooldredge & Steiner, 2016) Gaining respect impacts the quality of interactions and helps the facility run more smoothly.

While working in the education department, I met two staff members (teachers) who were kind and compassionate. So many of the officers were cruel and condescending to the women, but these men were not. Predictably, the women responded to their authority respectfully—and with what at times could almost be seen as friendship. I once asked one of these men what surprised him most about working with women (he had previously worked at a men's facility), and he responded that the male prisoners were better at accepting a simple "yes" or "no" from the staff. In contrast, women demand more details and explanations; they often pursue an issue to get their way rather than letting it drop. He said that the men accept definitive answers while the women see gray rather than black and white; things are not so simple for them.

In contrast to the respect earned by a few staff members, typical guard/convict interactions created tension and resistance. For example, one lieutenant issued a directive to a female inmate. She responded that the command didn't make sense. Irritated, he replied: "None of this makes any sense. . . . I'll do it, you'd probably just fuck it up anyway." Politely, the woman told him that he didn't need to talk to her that way. He then responded that he could do whatever the fuck he pleased, whenever he wanted.

Given the adversarial nature of most of our interactions with the guards, it was not surprising that retaliation by the women was common. I observed a number of instances firsthand and also heard stories about legendary (as defined by the women themselves) "set-ups" where officers had been hurt. For example, one of the popular retaliation "tricks" was to pour baby oil on the steps leading to a building or to a specific office, especially at night. On more than one occasion, a guard had fallen and was seriously injured. It does sound strange, as I type these words, to ask society to have compassion for those of us in prison, when the inmates themselves are not able to demonstrate compassion for the difficult job it must be to be an officer. I suppose the overall mean-spiritedness of the guards damages their authority and legitimacy in the eyes of the women, and I'm not sure either side believes they are doing anything that warrants correction.

> I often wonder if the guards/staff are deliberately cruel and purposefully insensitive. The mail room and the visitation room—the two most valued and coveted places for the women—are the areas in which we see the most horrific abuse of power and authority. Much of the humiliation and demeaning behavior is subtle, with faint hints of domination, but even the most understated actions feel heavy and very real, with devastating consequences for (on) the women. (journal entry)

> We'll get new guards in here at the end of the month (quarterlies). I'm not sure if I'm excited about that or not, it's a crap shoot knowing who or what you're going to get. Right now our main evening guard sucks. She's crazy (seriously). But at least it's not [Guard] because he's too busy fucking the inmates to notice what's going on in the units around him. (letter to my brother)

> I woke up this morning to the sound of the police searching lockers . . . nothing can ever be done respectfully, but I suppose, given the fact that many of the women *are* disrespectful, this does make sense. (journal entry)

THE ELDERLY

Forty years of harsh mandatory sentencing policies fueled by the drug war contributed to massive growth in the incarcerated population. There are an estimated 270,000 people aged 50 or older in state and federal prisons (Jefferson, 2018). Projections show that by 2030, one in three prisoners will be over the age of 55. Once released, aging prisoners do not qualify for Medicaid or Medicare. The increase in elderly prisoners has been a function of longer mandatory sentences, more life sentences, and more restrictive parole practices that limits the number of individuals being released from prison.

Prisons were not designed for age-related medical issues from arthritis to difficulty bathing to extensive medical attention required for strokes, emphysema, Alzheimer's, and cancer (Jefferson, 2018). Mental and physical declines are accelerated in prison; 40% of incarcerated older people have cognitive impairments including dementia. Because this population has extensive and costly medical needs, states are confronting complex, expensive repercussions from their sentencing practices. The healthcare costs of inmates 50 or older are 2 to 5 times higher than the costs for younger inmates. Recidivism research demonstrates that arrest rates are slightly more than 2% for people ages 50 to 65 years and almost zero for those older than 65—alleviating the risks of earlier release. Legislators and policy makers have been increasingly willing to consider early release for those older prisoners seen as posing low risks to public safety.

Despite strategies to release some elderly inmates, many states have not yet seen a decrease in their overall prison numbers, largely because the policies governing early releases are overly restrictive regarding eligibility (Chiu, 2010). Alabama instituted a medical furlough program in 2008, but only 39 people had been released by March 2016 (Silber, Shames, & Reid, 2017). In Texas, of 2,000 applications, only 176 were sent for review by the Board of Pardons and Parole, only 86 were approved for release. In federal prisons, 6% of more than 5,400 applications for compassionate releases were approved—about 5% of inmates who requested compassionate release died in custody (Chen, 2018).

> Thanks for asking about me, it's nice to talk. I've been here so long I feel like I'm invisible to everyone. . . . I was never in any trouble, my parents saw to that. Never did drugs or stole. Just bad at picking men I guess. It was a different generation back then, not like some of the stuff you see in here now. But then I finally had enough of my husband's "love" and couldn't take it anymore. I took care of him—you know what I mean [gently nudging me as I sat on the bunk next to her]. I'm in here forever, but he'll never touch me or our kids again. No one cared about me back then, and I 'spose no one

really cares about me now either. . . . I'm closer to 80 then
70; I'll be dead soon enough. (personal communication)

Female prisoners tend to be older than male prisoners
(Celinska & Sung, 2014). I had a very difficult time coming to
grips with the aging population of women around me. I was
stunned to see the number of women in wheelchairs, on
crutches, or moving slowly and unsteadily as time and prison
life took a toll on their bodies. As with the children and loved
ones in the women's lives, there was a sanctity about the
elderly around us, which was evident in the efforts of those
who worked hard to help others navigate the long walk across
the compound, or the stairs leading to most places inmates
were required to be. There were days that making a bunk
seemed an impossible task for the frail women stricken with
broken bones, arthritis, or simple fatigue.

MEDICAL SERVICES

Prison facilities for women typically lack proper medical
services despite the fact that women usually have more serious
health problems than men. A higher percentage of incarcerated
women report arthritis, asthma, cancer, heart problems, liver
problems, hepatitis, and sexually transmitted diseases (Clear et
al., 2019). The failure to provide women prisoners with the
most basic preventative medicine and procedures (ranging from
immunizations, breast cancer screening, and management of
chronic diseases) results in more serious health problems that
are exponentially more expensive to treat. It is unfortunate that
most in society do not realize poor medical care for those who
are incarcerated simply puts off and shifts costs to an already
overburdened community health care system once the prisoner
is released.

Incarcerated women also have a higher incidence of mental
health problems (Clear et al, 2019). Each year, about 4% of
women are pregnant when they are incarcerated. These are
high-risk pregnancies because most of the women are older than
35, have histories of drug abuse, and have had multiple abortions. All pregnant women need special medical and nutritional
resources. Women with mental illness and pregnant women
rarely receive the medical services they need while imprisoned.

All arrivals at the facility receive physicals including a blood test, a dental check, and vital signs. We answered questions about our health and various other related issues, but there was no real way to know if the women, including me, were being honest with the medical staff. It was so simple to lie about one's psychological well-being, or previous medical conditions. Although a urinalysis was required, no one monitored the process. We were sent to provide a sample and brought it back to the staff uncovered and unmarked. The women often joked about how easy it would be to substitute someone else's sample.

Access to medical care was extremely difficult for many women because the staff were often unavailable. When appointments were made (and kept), the staff often minimized inmate concerns, or blatantly ignored them. The serious health problems of most incarcerated women can be attributed to the increased likelihood of living in poverty, limited access to preventative medical care, poor nutrition, chemical dependency, or perhaps limited education on matters related to health. The majority of incarcerated women have never had access to health care because of homelessness, excessive mobility (constantly moving from one place to another), and lack of resources. Women in the criminal justice system often suffer from substance abuse, trauma due to sexual abuse and violence, and mental disorders (Celinska & Sung, 2014).

One of the main problems in women's prisons also has to do with the lack of skilled and available medical care (Owen et al., 2017). I attempted to go to "sick call" twice during my stay. Both times I waited in excess of 7 hours only to be turned away with a dismissive instruction to "go buy antihistamines at the commissary." A solution, by the way, that had absolutely nothing to do with my physical malady.

> I've had 3 periods this month. God they hurt. Being around so many women has messed up my cycle—it's unnatural and horribly painful. It's made worse when the guards don't regularly give out tampons or pads. I hate it here. (journal entry)

One medical employee was rumored to be a "caretaker of animals" from another country. I heard him tell a woman her uterus would grow back; he told another woman she was lactating because of a sinus infection.

Many prisons lack the gynecological/obstetrical services that most women require. They routinely fail to refer seriously ill inmates for treatment in a timely manner.

> Did you hear what they told us? They said that if they saw any of us helping her, they'd send us to the SHU. Can you believe that? She's got that scar all the way across her head that's still oozing, she can barely move. What's she supposed to do, lay there in her own piss and shit? How's she supposed to get to the dining hall, or even to the shower? That's bullshit man. [This comment was made by the bunkmate of a woman who had had emergency surgery to remove a brain tumor and was subsequently shipped back to our unit roughly a week after the operation.]

Several women died while I was there—none of old age. One was a 40-something Spanish lady in one of the bunks just down from mine. She complained often of stomach pains and discomfort, and her bunkmate said that she'd been asking for medical help for over a year, only to be routinely dismissed by the medical staff. Eventually her pain got so bad that she was taken to the hospital where she was diagnosed with cancer. Sadly, it was no longer treatable because it had progressed to the later stages; she died a short time later. The chapel held a memorial service for her, but there was no peace for those who knew her best, as her death was senseless and unnecessary. It was a tragedy that struck many throughout the prison.

> There was a strange feel to the compound this afternoon, and as we move into evening, the women seem restless and agitated. Today the chapel held services for the A. [the Spanish lady that recently died]—I couldn't go, I think it would be more than I could bear just now. (journal entry)

Stories of prolonged and undiagnosed illness could be told by a number of the women, particularly those who had been locked up for substantial periods of time. A woman in the bunk next to me said that several years before I arrived, another woman had been complaining of chest pains. She went to medical, only to be sent away with an asthma inhaler. She died later that evening of a heart attack. Senseless.

Chapter Eight

Rape by Any Other Name

The subject of sex in prison, particularly with regards to females, has largely been ignored in the incarceration literature. The rise in the number of female inmates over the years has changed the inmate prison culture, thus creating new challenges for prison administrators. The deprivation of sexual activity may cause extreme emotional, psychological, and even physical distress. There is often a link between sex and violent behavior in prison, and it is imperative that administrators develop prevention plans to make facilities safer for both inmates and correctional staff. Many of the women I met entered into same-sex liaisons to reduce stress, anxiety, and loneliness.

> I have been used and abused in prison by all those around me, both inmates and officers. Those in power use it to get their way with us. I am one of the silent victims that have been repeatedly touched and traumatized. I know in other people's eyes it may not seem so, but the abuse runs deeper here. What makes it worse is that I have to keep my mouth shut for fear of diesel therapy (being locked down and getting shipped away). (personal communication)

Nonconsensual sexual behavior is not about sexuality; it is about power, control, and manipulation. This makes coerced sexual activity a major policy issue for prison officials and a crucial area of concern for inmates. The fact that nonconsensual sex happens, and happens with regularity, in all U.S. correctional institutions is one of the most serious problems in the criminal justice system. While most people—from researchers, investigative reporters, prison officials, and legislators—agree it is a tragedy, there is wide disagreement on the nature and extent of the problem, the adequacy of legal protections afforded to female prisoners, and the appropriate responses by prison administrative officials.

> I was actually "approached" by a woman today—it didn't happen like I thought it would, but what do I know? I had no idea how these things happen in prison. I wasn't really offended, but I was quite surprised. I had pictures of [name of a man I was seeing prior to incarceration] all over the inside of my locker, but she didn't seem too concerned, she simply told me "if I get tired of dick, I should let her know." (journal entry)

A number of reports document the sexual abuse and exploitation of women prisoners at the hands of male correctional officers. Male prison employees use psychological coercion and/or physical force to gain sexual control over inmates. A national survey found that almost 5 percent of female inmates report being abused by another inmate and 2 percent by a staff member (Beck, Berzofsky, Caspar, & Krebs, 2013). Guards and other prison staff have almost unfettered control over prisoners. This power dynamic contributed to state and federal legislation that, as previously discussed, specifies sexual contact, regardless of consent, as criminal. Staff-on-inmate sexual misconduct covers a wide range of behaviors, from lewd remarks to voyeurism, to assault and rape. Few if any of these incidents are reported, and perpetrators rarely go to trial. Institutional workers cover for each other, and women who file complaints are offered little protection from vengeful guards. Because the situation persists, more than 40 states and the District of Columbia have passed laws criminalizing some types of staff sexual misconduct in prisons. However, not all sexual encounters in female institutions are unwanted. Rebecca Trammell (2009) conducted interviews with former female inmates; she found that some inmates fight over correctional officers as the only men in their lives.

LOVE IN PRISON

Estimates on the nature and extent of same-sex relationships in women's prisons differ based on varying institutional factors, including: distance from the prison to the female inmate's friends and relatives, the average length of time served (or to be served), and the policies that guide administrative decision making. It makes sense, especially to the people who have experienced the isolation of prison, that connections with other prisoners, whether physical or emotional, can mitigate the carceral experience.

> I actually managed to get a girlfriend in here, but when it came down to the sex part I backed out at the last minute. She said she would take care of me, but I don't like being controlled and obligated by people in here—if you know what I mean? (personal communication)

There was an aspect of "doing time" that focused solely on personal interactions and relationships. According to BOP guidelines, there is no "consensual sex" within any facility; all sexual activity is therefore considered sexual assault. The majority of the women did not take part in what often resembled juvenile, grade-school "coupling." However, there was a highly sexual atmosphere in the prison. Much of the arguing and many of the fights that took place were in response to transgressions in a relationship. The nature of the "interactions" ranged from sincere and "loving" (mock marriage ceremonies were not uncommon) to childish and self-indulgent. Public displays of affection between the female inmates were grounds for placement in the SHU for violating rule 205; however, a certain amount of physical interaction was tolerated and often times it was knowingly overlooked.

> Guess what I did? I stuck my tongue in a lady's kitty cat! It started out as a joke but I called her bluff. I didn't eat it, just licked it once. We started laughing but I got embarrassed and ran away. We were just having fun . . . it's tough to be horny in prison. (personal communication)

As I observed it, the relationships tended to fall into roughly four categories. I am certain there could be more, and I am sure that there is significant overlap and drift from one group to another. I do not pretend to know why the women behave as they do, falling into one relationship or another, nor do I presume to know how these relationships evolve or the dynamics that keep them going. The "associations" are not defined merely in sexual terms, or by sexual acts alone, because I witnessed a variety of relationships that had nothing to do with physical intimacy. Many of the Latino and Hispanic women, for example, developed exceptionally close "families" that included sisters, daughters, cousins, and even "nephews and sons." Some women assumed surprisingly masculine roles, including the adoption of male dress (even though we all wore the same uniform), hairstyle, or jobs and duties. This masculine function played a part in both intimate relationships, and the more domestic, family units. It is worth noting that race was not a social organizing factor; personal and sexual relationships among the women were often interracial and interethnic.

> Now, as far as the girlfriend thing . . . she left for camp ahead of me a month ago. We never got around to doing anything to seal the deal so I'm thinking it may not happen. Although, I *do* like her a lot. It's just that she's too nervous or whatever to start this and I won't simply because she has to do it to prove to me that's what she really wants. DAMN. Maybe I don't want the hassle of a relationship. I've got lots to figure out—sometimes I'm not so sure I know myself at all! Maybe my long bid (lengthy sentence) is simply taking its toll. (personal communication)

The first category was a predominantly heterosexual group. These women are typically married or have boyfriends at the time of their incarceration. They may be approached by other women in the facility, but they remain faithful to their male-female relationships. In my view, this appeared to be the majority of the women.

> The old man is still sort of around. I've got to tell you though, as of late, I'm feeling like I'm not going to wait for him (he is serving time in another state). Also, I think I can do better—not that I'm all that great, I'm a convict for God's sake, but still, I think maybe I deserve a little bit better than what I was settling for. (personal communication)

The second category consisted of lesbians, which was also a sizable group. These women had maintained monogamous relationships with same-sex partners on the outside and will most likely continue to do so after release. They may at times become involved in a relationship while incarcerated; being locked up has not directly impacted their sexuality.

The third category was heterosexual women who became involved with women while incarcerated. These women were either married to men or had been in relationships with men on the outside. For reasons such as companionship, intimacy, and the fear of alienation/loneliness associated with long-term sentences, they become involved with other incarcerated females. The convicts referred to this as "gay for the stay."

The final grouping consisted of women who participated in "bull-dagging." These relationships were characterized by multiple partners. They included the swapping of partners, and sometimes forced/coerced sexual activity/favors. Typically, one woman was dominant; the other(s) would work, cook, clean, fight, and perform sexual favors for the one in charge.

> Did you hear what they did to [inmate name] in the stall? They tore her up inside. Of course the Hen (reference to one of the sexually abusive female inmates) said she wanted it, asked for it even. But you and I know that ain't true. Those bull-daggers don't play. (personal communication)

> It's always been hard for me to be intimate. I had that gang thing (referring to a gang rape that took place when she was a teenager), and then, being a prostitute, but that's not real intimacy, and that's what scares me! I'm afraid to be touched. I haven't been touched in years, I don't know that I've ever really *enjoyed* being touched. I'm not sure I know what that's like. (personal communication)

The psychology department had a "meditation room." The idea was that inmates could go there to spend some time alone, to enjoy a bit of peace and quiet. To be able to go to the room, we had to have earned the privilege—for example, no disciplinary write-ups for a while, an educational success, or some therapeutic achievement. The room wasn't much, but hiding out in it became one of the things I looked forward to most. The small dimly lit room had a comfortable leather recliner; there was also a soft, cozy blanket and an overstuffed pillow. The chair was strategically positioned so that anyone walking by could not see it through the small window in the door. There was also a small tape deck and a decent selection of music suitable for meditation—from Bach to Mozart, Celtic to Gregorian chant music. The women were allowed one hour alone in this room; some would sleep, some would read, some would reflect, and I am told that many would masturbate.

> That reminds me, [inmate name] gave me a 10" cock for my b-day! She made it out of red jolly-ranchers with now & laters on the inside. Cool huh? Can't you just picture me

up on my bunk licking and sucking that huge cock? I'll end up with a stack of shots, alone in the SHU, and no cock. Guess I better hide it. (personal communication)

As previously mentioned, the sexually charged nature of the facility could not be ignored. Blatant sexuality was all around us—from the making and flaunting of dildos by the inmates to the guards who would intentionally display the toys after confiscation. In one of the unit offices, the guards had a wall-mounted shadowbox where they placed the confiscated items. During the day the women were chastised, written up, and punished for sexual expressions; at night, often with no attempt at secrecy, guards and inmates traded sex for favors. It was offensive to newcomers like me, but others expected and accepted the behavior, having seen far worse during their years of incarceration.

This week they started the trial against the 2 officers who didn't plea out. They had the fucking nerve to put the women's names on the callout sheets. [Callout sheets are the system of notifying the inmate of an appointment with their case worker, therapist, etc.] They fucking put COURT right there in black and white for the women who were being called to testify. That's such bullshit, such messiness. You know this would never happen in a men's prison—shit like that wouldn't happen. People would die. But here in fantasy prison, anything is possible. (personal communication)

Many of the women walked around the units naked, in overtly sexual ways—maybe they had simply gotten used to their bodies no longer being their own, or perhaps they'd lost pride in who they were, or maybe it was about finding control—displaying their bodies first, and on their terms, without being asked and without shame. Privacy was definitely something we gave up once we were sent to prison; modesty no longer seemed to exist. There was nowhere to hide when we changed our clothes. It seemed silly to even try. I'm not sure how prison officials could not see this as victimization; perhaps they do, and they simply don't care. We were victimized at every turn—the strip searches and cavity explorations we endured in the name of safety, the constant stream of profanity-laced threats, the withholding of necessities like tampons, and the watching of women showering and using the restroom. I reiterate my statement from the preface that I do not want to minimize the harm done by the women in the commission of their crimes. But I also cannot fathom how our repeated degradation and humiliation (and sexual assault) is/can be justified under the guise of "paying our debts."

> On a humorous note—the gal across the bunk from me is visibly upset with me and 1 other lady down the aisle because we are still up and awake! She is one of the women who has sex with guards—he's one of the biggest jackasses (and notably one of the guards who ultimately got caught up in the sex for drugs scandal). Strangely enough, they're very blatant about the relationships during the day; I'm really quite surprised they care one way or another that we see it at night! (letter to my brother)
> [A sad note regarding the woman having sex with the guard; shortly after my release, I found out she became pregnant (after having been incarcerated for 5 years). Rather than disciplining the officer, she was packed up and shipped off to another facility.]

There were a significant number of women who spent their days communicating with men on the outside through the various pen pal websites. On rare occasions, a woman could have access to the internet through the computer or business courses that were sometimes taught. On other occasions, relatives of the women would "arrange the relationships" for them. The letter-writing and phone calls included men in prisons as well; many of them were knowingly involved with more than one woman. It was not uncommon for the women to send provocative pictures of themselves (or with another woman) or to write erotic letters (known as "900" letters). Both activities were done in exchange for money placed in their accounts.

A new woman in class talked about being in the SHU for 8 months, which was unusual for FCI. We were curious to learn what she had done; like a bunch of teenagers, we anxiously waited to hear the salacious details. Her daughter posted a picture of the woman at age 18 on the internet with the caption "I'm in prison, I'm lonely, would you like to write me?" When men wrote to her, she replied that the pens, pencils, paper, stamps, and envelopes for correspondence cost $50 per month in the commissary. She enclosed a commissary sheet so that they would see the prices. The men, many of them lonely and looking for someone to chat with, would eagerly post money in her commissary account. She had roughly $63,000 in her commissary account when the guard in her unit began complaining about the volume of mail she received. The feds put her in the hole during their investigation and went through every letter she wrote—an obviously time-consuming project—but to their chagrin there was no evidence of anything illegal. She never solicited money, and she was very careful about the way she worded her letter. Prison officials ultimately had to release her from the SHU.

> The warden gave her the "don't get too much mail" speech—whatever! And as if that wasn't funny enough, because I'm now at the point where I do love it if someone gets one over "the man," she's counter-sued the facility for her attorney fees. She hired an attorney from her home state while she was going through this, and now she wants the government to pay—I'm not sure how this will all pan out, but you've got to love her for trying! (letter to my brother)

FOR ALL THE WRONG REASONS

> Would you believe she gave him a blowjob for a Big Mac? He offers it to her all the time. I guess it's fine if the other women don't care. (personal communication)

One evening as I was preparing for commissary night, I had a revelation of sorts. For the first time in months, I'd found myself concerned with my personal appearance (hair, clothing, and makeup). I was also overcome with an almost-giddy feeling of eagerness to get out on the compound. It took me some time to realize why, and further, to accept what this might have meant. I wasn't sure I really wanted to write about this, or openly admit to what I was feeling at the time, but I think it's important for the reader to know how easily, and perhaps harmlessly, some relationships can develop and evolve in prison. One of the men that worked in "the store" had become overly friendly with me. He had a nickname for me and generally had longer-than-normal conversations with me. At times he would ask about my day, or my purchases, or even about my friends and family. I hadn't thought much about it until that night. What surprised me was that I wasn't excited for the replenishing of hygiene supplies, or for seeing other friends, or even for extra snacks. Oddly enough, I was *looking forward* to seeing "him." I have been very critical of the sexual relationships I witnessed and heard about throughout my sentence. Like many of the other things I initially did not understand (the camaraderie, the putting on makeup and getting dressed, etc.), I now was beginning to have a vague understanding of how and why some of the relationships begin. It began to make sense to me, particularly amidst the chaos we were living. In times of extraordinary stress, being held tightly in the safety and comfort of someone's arms was far better than being huddled alone in the corner of one's bunk.

I am by no means condoning these sexual relationships and blatant staff-inmate affairs, but I think each person needs to be in a certain position to be able to truly comprehend it—and to pass judgment on it. We spend most of our days (and nights) being told how useless we are and how insignificant we are, and this seems to magnify the most subtle or harmless remarks (both good and bad). I've mentioned this several times throughout the book, but it's about validation—regardless of whether it is for the "right" reason (friendship versus manipulation). I cannot speak for others; all I have to go on is my own experience. For me it was about someone (particularly a man) acknowledging that I am something other than a number. Were his intentions "honorable"? I don't know. I doubt it, but I enjoyed (and indeed looked forward to) the attention nonetheless. Could it have been about manipulation? Absolutely. I suppose at the time, it simply didn't matter to me. I felt ugly, both inside and outside, and so damaged that even the smallest of gestures diminished the ugliness momentarily. I know what others might be thinking, but it's too easy to say it's just about "flirting." For me anyway, it was something far deeper. It was about reaffirming one's sexuality; it was about feeling valued; and it was about feeling less broken.

Some of the relationships between inmates and officers start out with flirtation and then escalate into some sort of sexual relationship. According to BOP, we cannot consent; therefore, everything is considered sexual assault. Many women seem to get to a point where they are willing to ignore the fact that they are being taken advantage of in exchange for items that they could easily and cheaply buy outside the prison walls. Guards bring all sorts of things into the facility—lingerie, makeup, drugs and alcohol, even fast food. Having said this, there are (were) far too many instances of forcible rape and sexual coercion at FCI Tallahassee, and I would assume this abuse occurs at other facilities with the same regularity. Why these abuses take place depends on so many variables: the women involved, the staff, the facility, the time and/or location, the motivations, etc. All I can offer is my own interpretation, and as with most things in prison, it is simply not enough to say one group is right and the other is wrong. That sort of black and white thinking does not exist in prison. To survive, with even a modicum of sanity, we chose to live in shades of gray.

> B. is on her bunk yammering about the sex she just had in the bathroom stall. I struggle to understand how she uses terms like romance and love. How in *the hell* does that happen here? (journal entry)

It sounds cliché to say that I was transformed by this experience, but I was (and continue to be) in more ways than I ever could have predicted. These changes followed me into civilian life—into my teaching, my community service work, and even into my personal life. Over the course of my criminal justice journey—from arrest to release—I experienced fear, embarrassment, humiliation, and even joy. Through all this, however, it is the sexually abusive nature of the prison and the impact on the lives of the women that challenged me most. Much like the evolution of my pre-prison conservative ideology, living with and sharing in the lives of these women altered my perspective on the intimate relationship dynamics and the sexual activities that shaped the culture of the prison. The violence and/or crimes perpetrated by the women must certainly not be ignored, but I *saw* them, often at their most vulnerable, and I *felt* their distress, and I *experienced* their hopelessness. How could I not be changed?

This was a difficult section for me to write. It would not be accurate (or helpful) to assert that all prison staff and/or guards are abusive or malicious. It would be equally untrue to suggest that none of the female inmates are complicit in the turmoil and chaos of the prison. Each case (each woman) has a story to be told. Some are complicated; most are not. These women deserve acknowledgment, humane treatment, and to be released from prison better off than when they arrived.

> Apparently [inmate] is being sent to Carswell (a medical facility/prison in Texas), it would be simply cruel to leave her in the SHU for the remainder of her pregnancy. (letter to my brother)

Sexual Misconduct

The sexual abuse of women in prison has been a problem since women were first incarcerated in this country and was one of the reasons behind the movement to separate incarcerated men and women. The lack of research on the sexual coercion that takes place in prison reflects the lack of overall awareness of the problem, misperceptions (by the public, media, and scholars) about the nature of prison sexual coercion, and hardened attitudes toward prisoners that they deserve whatever happens to them.

Carceral agencies routinely require their staff to perform strip searches, body cavity searches, and nonconsensual medical interventions on prisoners—acts that have a great deal in common with sexual violence. As evidenced by the ruling about the Illinois women's prison, the courts are reluctant to establish limits to these procedures that are portrayed as necessary for institutional safety.

The Prison Rape Elimination Act (PREA) was implemented in 2003. It requires the collection of national statistics on prison sexual victimization based on a scientific sample of not less than 10% of all federal, state, and county detention facilities (Bureau of Justice Statistics, 2018). The government collects statistics from prison administrators, and it conducts anonymous surveys of inmates (Santo, 2018). PREA included a requirement to develop national standards for the prevention, detection, and response to prison rape. The standards were issued in 2012 and require correctional facilities to educate staff and inmates on sexual victimization and to refer all allegations of sexual victimization for investigation (Rantala, 2018). In 2015, correctional administrators reported 24,661 allegations of sexual victimization, compared to 8,768 allegations in 2011. There were 1,473 substantiated allegations in 2015. Legally, any sexual contact between corrections officers and the incarcerated people in their charge is rape, which makes the low number of substantiations particularly disturbing (Leonard, 2017).

The adult correctional authorities report on sexual victimization for 2012-2015 (released in 2018) did not include the gender of alleged victims and perpetrators, which had been included in the previous report. Between 2009 and 2011, women were about 7% of all state and federal prison inmates but accounted for 22% of inmate-on-inmate victims and 33% of staff-on-inmate victims (Beck, et al., 2013). In local jails, women were 13% of the inmates but 27% of the victims (67% of all staff-on-inmate victimization).

The Bureau of Justice Statistics (BJS) estimates that more than 200,000 inmates are sexually abused in detention facilities annually (Santo, 2018). Vulnerabilities that exist in the free world are magnified in the penal system (Bruenig, 2015). Incarcerated inmates with mental health problems and LGBTQ inmates are at higher risk for sexual abuse in adult facilities. The 2011-2012 BJS report found that 32 people per 1,000 were sexually abused in jail; 40 people per 1,000 were sexually abused in prison; and 95 juveniles per 1,000 were sexually abused in detention facilities. In contrast, the rate of rape and sexual assault in society was 1.3 per 1,000—a prisoner is roughly 30 times more likely to be the victim of a sexual assault.

Despite the mandates of PREA, the legislation is only as effective as it is allowed to be (Bruenig, 2015). It is difficult to imagine the public being indifferent to similar legislation applied to any other population. "We have become a culture that tolerates and potentially lauds the rape and sexual exploitation of hundreds of thousands of people every year, many of them minors, mothers, mentally ill. Why?" (p. 7).

Official statistics cannot capture the victims who do not report misconduct. The coercive power imbalance between guard and prisoner silences victims. Prisoners cannot escape a rapist (Stannow, 2017). Assailants have the keys to cells, and they have the authority to order victims to remote parts of a facility. After an assault, victims cannot call a hotline, confide in family members, or even go for a walk. Victims fear retaliation—whether violent or regular harassment. Inmates may find their mail is not delivered, their cells are searched repeatedly, or visitors may wait hours before being admitted (Leonard, 2017). A persistent myth is that other inmates are chiefly responsible for the sexual violence inflicted on prisoners (Bruenig, 2015). However, inmates in state and federal prisons and local jails all reported greater rates of sexual victimization involving staff.

Disagreement about the extent of the problem exists, as does the availability and efficacy of legal protections for inmates and responses by correctional officials that would allow prisoners to feel safe reporting abuse. The Prison Litigation Reform Act (PLRA) requires prisoners to exhaust all administrative remedies before filing suit in federal court to challenge prison abuses. As a result, victims must report their abuse to the people committing or facilitating the abuse before seeking legal remedies. Lovissa Stannow is the executive director of Just Detention International, the leading advocacy organization. While the number of allegations reported increased after the new national standards, the vast majority were determined to be false or there was not enough evidence to decide (Santo, 2018). Stannow said prisoners have nothing to gain from filing false reports and that corrections officials often begin with the assumption that the report against a colleague is false; there is a strong tendency to close ranks.

Diana Block is a founding member of the California Coalition for Women Prisoners. She remarked on the positions of men with absolute power over a captive population. All of the dynamics of sexism and sexual violence prevalent in society carry over to conduct and behaviors in prisons where victims have very little protection or recourse (Endicott, 2018). In the context of prison, sexual harassment becomes even more violent, humiliating, and dehumanizing because it is seen as part of the punishment for committing a crime. The prison is a closed system. To report staff misconduct, prisoners can file an administrative appeal (a 602) to request an investigation, but the filing is with coworkers of the people who committed the abuse.

Historically, incarcerated women in the United States have experienced high levels of sexual advances, coercion, and harassment by staff. These behaviors are broadly considered sexual misconduct and range from sexual assault to sexual abuse to obscenity and unreasonable invasion of privacy, to romantic conversations and/or gestures between a prisoner and staff members. This does not represent the entire list of behaviors considered sexual misconduct, but they represent situations that I witnessed, and experienced firsthand. As mentioned several times in the text, the majority of the women have pre-prison histories that include sexual and physical violence, often coupled with addictions and mental health concerns. Experiencing the unwanted (often aggressive and coerced) sexual behaviors of someone working in the correctional facility compounds the trauma.

It is important to note that even in situations when sexual relations do not involve the overt use or threat of force, the

relationship is not one where both parties are equal. When I
was incarcerated, I saw this played out a number of times. The
officer always had the upper hand—regardless of who initiated
the relationship. The relationship was always on his terms. If a
woman wanted to end the relationship, he could use his
authority to manipulate her into staying with him. This abuse
of power took a variety of forms, from outright physical abuse
to more subtle forms of coercion. Given the significant number
of women who report being physically and/or sexually abused
prior to incarceration, experiencing sexual abuse in prison can
compound the psychological damage of serving time. Many
women in the criminal justice system are marginalized members of society, which increases their vulnerability to those in
powerful positions of those at the facility.

The reasons why incarcerated women might not report the
sexual misconduct they experience mirror the reasons of
women on the outside. We discussed retaliation earlier—a very
real and frequent occurrence in prison. The victim may think
she won't be believed by prison officials. In addition, the chain
of command may mean that complaints must be submitted to
the very officers who committed the abuse. Some female prisoners may have consented to a relationship initially, and they
expect their complaints will be dismissed for that reason. Incarceration of a large number of women, particularly women with
histories of trauma, in a closed institution with staff who have
considerable power over them, creates a context of vulnerability
and sometimes terrifying conditions. Some facilities may have
instituted policies and procedures to protect inmates, in combination with improved training and selection of officers that
result in fewer cases of sexual misconduct. Tallahassee was not
one of those places (at least not at the time).

> So, [inmate name] was sent to the SHU (she's the newest
> pregnant gal), and get this, the guard responsible wasn't
> fired! Granted, in a number of these cases, the women con-
> sented to the sex, but the fact that the relationships go on
> without response (repercussions) simply confirms the less
> worthy way in which people see us (convicts). He worked
> (if by *work* you mean reclining on the bunks of certain
> women for most of the evening or standing in one place in
> the back—God forbid something bad happens to the other
> 240 women) in our unit last night, wedding ring and all.
> *Clearly* concerned with his job and the morality of the situ-

ation, he's now making time with several other women. What an asshole! (letter to my brother)

This place is fucking crazy! I think I already mentioned the fact that Officer J. [guard] was back . . . all charges dropped, working up front in the admin area. There's some talk that his attorney made deals with other inmates for information. How keeping J. benefits BOP is beyond me, maybe it's to avoid publicity. (letter to my brother)

Chapter Nine

"Ain't That Some Shit?"

Prison conditions foster hate, violence, addiction, and self-loathing, ironically many of the same toxic circumstances that propel an offender to engage in criminal activity in the first place. It makes mean people meaner and weak people weaker. In my experience, it is a rare occasion when prison changes an individual's life for the better. One major cause of the extraordinary incarceration rate in the United States is the punitive ideology of harsh sentencing laws and restrictive release mechanisms. I would also suggest that there is an undercurrent of contempt directed at those who lack the resources and opportunities to achieve (much less sustain) positive change.

TOXIC ENVIRONMENT

Many of the women I talked with shared eerily similar and frightening stories of emotional, physical, and sexual abuse prior to incarceration. Most of the women turned to drugs or alcohol in an attempt to assuage the pain. Using illicit drugs and living on the streets typically meant engaging in prostitution or petty crimes to survive. It is an unfortunate reality that many of these women end up in the custody of a system ill-equipped to deal with the physical and emotional scars that addiction and abuse leave behind. Criminalizing women in these situations seems cruel and unwarranted, and completely counterproductive if the goals of the system are to "correct." Our current criminal justice system appears to have a callous disregard for the individual needs of the people, particularly the women, in its custody.

The amount of sexual activity and abuse in women's prisons is impossible to quantify. Despite the research conducted by
state and federal authorities, we still know very little about the
sexual abuse that takes place in many of this country's correctional facilities. One of the main challenges has to do with what
does and does not count as abuse (beyond the BOP's definition
of abuse). In dealing with the issue of inmate sexual assault,
one must be aware that the definition of what this actually
means is itself a problem.

The public's overall lack of concern for inmate abuse
accounts for the lack of legislative action to protect vulnerable
prisoners. Society takes seriously allegations of sexual abuse in
our communities, but the perception remains that criminals are
less worthy of the same protection and safety. Personal experience and years of engaging in conversations with women who
have endured the unfettered abuse illuminates the frequency of
harassment—a sad and constant reminder of how little power
inmates have once they begin serving their time.

The women at FCI Tallahassee—both inmate and officer—
could often be heard complaining about sexual abuse by the
male guards. Stories were often told of women being impreg-
nated by guards (and sometimes, administrative staff). Some of
these pregnancies resulted in abortions; other women gave
birth while in prison. Many of the women feared physical and
sexual abuse at the hands of the officers. If a woman reported
being coerced into sex, she was likely to face some sort of retribution, including termination of visits or phone calls, threats to
family, or removal of personal possessions. On the rare occasion
that these crimes were reported, the officer received only minimal sanctions. The most severe punishment was being sent to
the male detention facility or given probation. In other cases,
guards served no prison time despite admitting guilt. Frequently, the abuse resulted in a misdemeanor charge.

I am certain that many of the people working in prisons,
and the corrections field as a whole, are professionals who do
nothing wrong. There were some officers and staff I met who
were kind and professional, but there were not very many of
them. Hiring more female staff plus restrictions on men from
entering where women undress and from performing pat-
downs and strip searches would be one way to help women feel
safer while they are locked up. However, having unsupervised

males in female facilities and giving them full access to females at night—or in intimate situations (women changing clothes, showering, strip searches)—creates an environment conducive to sexual abuse. In these settings, outright violation of women's privacy by officers amounts to a regular part of life for female inmates. The abusive behaviors I witnessed (and experienced) often included hand and/or body gestures mimicking sexual acts, derogatory sexual comments to (and about) the women, and unwanted physical contact that included brushing against a woman's breasts, grabbing her buttocks, or forcing a female inmate to touch the officer's groin.

THE FCI INCIDENT

There are complex issues surrounding sexual safety in prison—staffing issues related to gender, for example, as well as legitimate security concerns and the protection of inmate safety and privacy. Sexual relations between staff/guards and prisoners were certainly not uncommon; I have been very open about that throughout this book. The outcome of the FCI investigation had such devastating and lasting consequences, that I decided to devote a chapter to it. Accounts of the incident vary somewhat depending on the source, but most of the media reports portrayed the investigation reasonably and realistically. According to both media and inmate sources, the federal investigation of the identified officers took place over the course of several years. In hindsight, it appears that the prison administration (at least some administrators) were aware of the abuse. On some level it is understandable that the prison allowed the guards to remain in their positions in the interest of "building a stronger case" against them—however this plan unfortunately subjected the female prisoners to additional unnecessary abuse.

> Holy shit! Turn on the news—check CNN or one of the other big new stations! Check the news! Check out what's going on in Tallahassee. *Ain't that some shit?* You have to call me back! Oh my God, please call me. (Message left on my phone by a former FCI inmate)

The charges against the FCI officers included exchanging contraband, specifically drugs, alcohol, and money, for sex with the female inmates. They were also charged with attempting to bribe and intimidate the women into keeping quiet about the abuse. Threatening to ship a woman to another facility even farther away from family was a tactic often utilized by an officer in an attempt to keep her from discussing the situation. The guards also monitored the women's phone calls for the purpose of intimidating and identifying women who were disclosing the criminal conduct to other persons. I was surprised that I was never subjected to intimidation or retaliation because I made a number of blatant accusations on the phone and in many of my letters (much to my brother's dismay).

To facilitate the abusive relationships, the guards frequently switched duty assignments. This allowed them to be in total control of the women and their day-to-day interactions. The guards received money from the women, their family members, and their associates in exchange for the goods the officers smuggled into the prison. In an attempt to hide what was going on, some officers would hide the various items in sections of the prison easily accessible by the women. Other times, there were no attempts made to hide the transactions. Many of the women, and indeed the officers they were involved with, were not particularly shy about the food, alcohol, clothing (typically lingerie), or other illegal items they brought into our unit. Despite officers' requests to keep relationships secret, the women could often be heard discussing sexual encounters in graphic detail.

On June 21, 2006, federal agents arrived to serve warrants on six guards charged in the exchange of contraband for sex. One of the guards had smuggled a gun into the facility. He wounded an arresting agent, ran to the parking lot, and engaged in a shoot-out with the other agents. The guard and an agent died. I had already been released; this chapter is based on news reports, the recollection of a staff member, and conversations with some of the women incarcerated when the incident occurred.

Vincent Johnson, Alfred Barnes, and E. Lavon Spence pled guilty to mail fraud. Spence and Barnes also admitted to having sex with prisoners in exchange for contraband, while Johnson claimed he only pressured a prisoner not to cooperate with officials in the investigation. Gregory Dixon was convicted by a jury on three counts of bribery and conspiracy to accept illegal gratuities. The same jury convicted Alan Moore of tampering with a witness, conspiracy to accept illegal gratuities, and accepting an illegal gratuity. During the trial, U.S. District Judge Robert Hinkle dismissed the most serious charges against Dixon and Moore, and the jury acquitted both of conspiracy to commit bribery.

Problems of harassment and abuse at FCI Tallahassee are similar to other federal prisons. As previously mentioned, the bribery, sexual abuse, and other crimes committed by prison guards are a regular occurrence in a women's correctional facility. For a federal guard to have sex with a prisoner is a federal crime punishable by up to 15 years in prison. Sadly, as the research in this book makes abundantly clear, prosecutors rarely file felony charges against federal prison guards who rape prisoners in their custody. In previous chapters I have discussed the fact that some women do willingly enter into sexual relationships with prison staff. With FCI Tallahassee, as with all other correctional institutions, consent is not a defense. It was a travesty that the mail fraud and bribery-related charges were punished more severely than the sexual abuse of prisoners under supervision by those guards. At the time the crimes occurred, sexual abuse was only a misdemeanor (Clarke, 2007).

The shooting made headlines. Public and media interest in the sexual abuse, if it existed at all, quickly faded. The five guards who stood trial received ridiculously light sentences; the outcomes were barely mentioned in the national press. Spence received a year of home detention, plus three years of probation. Dixon, Moore, and Barnes received one-year prison sentences, and Johnson was sentenced to a year of probation, a sentence mitigated in part because he shielded a federal agent during the shoot-out. The female prisoners in Tallahassee didn't fare quite as well. Right after the shooting, the women's facility was locked down. For several days, the women were denied all visits and phone calls. "I'm so glad I'm headed for a camp," one of the women stressed, "maybe there we're simply allowed to do our time without having to worry about the people who supervise us."

Assessing blame is complicated, as chapter 8 illustrates. Inmate/staff relationships occur all the time despite prohibition. Do the women share responsibility? Perhaps. Is it something that can be stopped? Probably not. I don't know what the answer is (or should be), or even how the problems can be resolved. What I *do* know, is that the correctional system needs transparency and legitimate oversight. Officials need to stop the monthly notice prior to a facility's inspection; these should be done randomly, at night, and with no warning. This might well be the only way prison officials will truly know what takes places behind closed doors and when the lights go out.

The deadly events led to the installation of metal detectors that guards must now pass through and an X-ray machine that monitors the bags they bring into the facility.

> You know how rumors fly in here, but we know far more than people like to give us credit for—guess because we're criminals, we're automatically stupid. Poor decision makers? Yes. Stupid? No. (ok, some are.) The officers that are still here, whether dirty or not, appear nervous. With good reason. I assume this is far from over. It's not like this is something new. C'mon, it's happening in the men's prisons too. My husband tells some pretty horrific stories about [name of a men's prison]. Their stuff's not so much for sex, but more extortion for money. The media makes it out to look like the girls here were victims. Most of these women are anything but! They were just doing what they do best—manipulating men into getting what they want! (personal communication)

Chapter Ten

Society and Its Ex-Cons

Incarceration plays an extraordinary role in creating and maintaining a permanent underclass in this country, largely defined by race and income (Shelden & Vasiliev, 2018). Incarceration patterns deeply affect the economic and social development of communities. Breaking the cycle of poverty, abuse, and incarceration requires a reallocation of resources, to support the successful reintegration of people returning from prison, which would improve public safety and limit further destabilization of marginalized families and communities. In the 6 months that I was incarcerated, it struck me that the misery of so many women could be alleviated by some very simple ideas: decrease the number of women in prison, recognize the value of quality (and realistic) rehabilitative programming efforts, and decrease the suffering experienced daily in prison.

As with much of the criminal justice system, particularly when it comes to correctional practices, most policies and program related to reentry and reintegration were created based on studies that focused on male populations. The research makes clear, however, that women have a significantly higher need for services than men, and reentry support should be geared to the particular needs of justice-involved women (Sawyer, 2019). One in eight people released from prison annually are women, resulting in 81,000 women who need services to increase opportunities for successful reentry. Another 1.8 million women are released from local jails.

Concentrated Incarceration

In his book *Imprisoning Communities*, Todd Clear (2007) discusses the problem of concentrated incarceration. "The concentration of imprisonment of young men from disadvantaged places has grown to such a point that it is now a bedrock experience, a force that affects families and children, institutions and businesses, social groups and interpersonal relationships (p. 3). Clear's overarching point is that imprisonment has grown to the point that it now amplifies the very behaviors and social problems it was designed to eliminate. Throughout this book I have talked often about disadvantaged neighborhoods, family fragmentation, the lack of educational and employment opportunities, and the generational nature of poverty, violence, and abuse that plague the lives of many of the women I met during my carceral experience (as well as the women I met prior to and following my incarceration). If we as a society do nothing to alter disadvantages, releasing prisoners to these failing communities increases the likelihood of continued self-destructive behaviors and crime.

> I will be leaving in about 6 months and I'm so nervous and scared! For so long I have lived on the streets and I have lived a certain lifestyle, I don't want to fail at living righteously and safely in the future. My children mean the world to me, though I barely know them now. Putting my life back together will be a lifelong struggle because I have to rise above what others in my family could not. My life has never really been together anyway. I think I will always have to deal with the scars inside, of abuse in the past. What if I can't be strong? What if my desire to succeed simply isn't enough? What do I do then? (personal communication)

> I know it's been hard for you to tell people about your past, but I also know that people who are disturbed by it are not worth knowing! No person is defined by the worst or greatest moment of their life. To do so renders them stagnant. Stop selling yourself short. The true measure of a person is what's in the heart. In you beats the heart of a beautiful, intelligent, creative, loving, compassionate woman. Embrace the struggles you're having, through them will come your strength. You are the voice of truth—a counterbalance on the scale of life against the weight of injustice, uneducated, and naïve beliefs in our society. I feel and share your pain and I

weep with you and for you. I am certain I will soon feel the same public shame and weakness as you. My time here is almost up but do know that you will always have my unconditional love, undying loyalty, and unending commitment. Look deep inside my sister and you will see what God and I already know about you. (personal communication)

In addition to whatever emotional scars a woman takes with her following release, reentering society presents a number of serious problems—frequently the same problems that led to incarceration, compounded by a criminal conviction and the resentment fueled by that label. These women will continue to struggle with mental and/or physical illness, lacking the health care that decent and stable employment might provide for them. Many of these women have limited educational backgrounds that affect the potential for new career choices. So many women have been (and continue to be) locked up for drug crimes, which means that they will be denied public assistance after release. Prison policies overlook the basic idea that you cannot change prisoners without simultaneously changing the communities where they will return.

Women released from prison face a challenge finding safe and stable housing. If there are other members of the family with felony convictions, they will be barred from associating with them, which exacerbates already strained family relations. They may face further ostracism by their communities, including landlords who can deny rentals based on the felony conviction. Once convicted of a crime, women often lose custody of their children. Getting them back is a long and arduous process, plus the expense of a lawyer. Released prisoners face readjustment to changed surroundings, to technology with which they are unfamiliar, and to temptations in the neighborhoods where their drug use or criminal activity took place. It's easy to understand why so many women are eventually reincarcerated.

I had numerous conversations with women serving lengthy sentences. Most had very similar answers when asked about their futures—they couldn't afford to look forward. They live day to day, moment to moment. For some, the only hope is for renewed parole options (alternative release mechanisms); still others hope for nothing at all. As long as society views human beings as disposable, we are destined to continue to treat them not as people, but as chattel—numbered, counted, and stacked in cages.

Thank you for your last letter, I so look forward to them. Absolutely! You are free to use any of my poems however you'd like, as well as anything else we may discuss. I trust you, as you surely know. I am certain that your book will be well received, but likely more by those who have walked this path at some time. No one can understand but someone who has lived through it. Cliché as it sounds, it is so very true. If nothing else, it will be good for you. I too will soon face the struggle of getting out and trying to pick up the pieces of my shattered life. (personal communication)

I am not condoning or minimizing the crimes committed by women, or the harm caused. Rather, I challenge the very philosophy of *why* we punish in the first place. If our larger goal, as a society, is to protect our communities and limit the victimizations of others, logic would dictate that we "level the playing field" with regards to the criminogenic factors that increase the likelihood that someone will engage in criminal behavior. The majority of the women I met had very similar pathways into crime. There was a common theme in their stories that explained crimes as a mechanism for survival, providing for their children, coping with early life trauma, and/or the dependency on a man who was far more entrenched in serious criminal behaviors. Many of these women lived in the margins of society, cycling in and out of homelessness, struggling with mental health issues, spending time with abusive partners, and dealing with substance addiction—an explosive combination of dynamics that too often lead to prison.

Of course, free will is a factor, as is accountability. But perhaps if we took the time to examine the entirety of crime(s) committed—with less self-righteous condemnation—we might understand the unwinnable situations that so many incarcerated individuals face. Less expensive alternatives do exist (day reporting centers, community service, and the like). Although still punishment, these alternatives can help "correct" the decision making and behaviors of those who commit crime. We *must* find more humane answers that do not include the brutality and humiliation that comes with an already painful prison sentence.

I agree with you that the word "reentry" seems inappropriate as many of these women move back into society. It does indeed apply to a small portion of us (perhaps the two of us, for example), I think there may be a better word to really capture what it means to go from marginalized citizen to prison to marginalized citizen again. I'm not sure why anyone would think that simply being in prison somehow makes people better. I have however, met many women who are working for UNICOR (call center) here and it is work they have never known before and they are very good at it . . . so it is giving them confidence and also some skill in a field they might otherwise not have known. Their reentry will be easier than for others who are no better for their time here (and in fact, much worse for their time and the stigma that will follow them back into reality). (personal communication)

RELEASE INTO THE COMMUNITY

Prison definitely doesn't rehabilitate you. Being here has made me hateful. Being here has made me not care about the next person and has made me realize how I don't really give a damn about nothing. (personal communication)

What society expects from the corrected offender and what society actually allows are two very different things. Inmates released today will be less prepared for the life that awaits them on the outside. They will be offered less assistance in their reintegration, and they will face the increasing likelihood of being returned to prison for parole violations or new crimes. Post-prison supervision is more stringent than probation supervision; parolees have a 20% higher chance of being returned to prison within five years compared to probationers (Harding, Morenoff, Nguyen, & Bushway, 2017). Approximately 30% of new prison admissions are for technical violations (i.e. failure to report to parole officers, failure to complete required program, substance abuse, changing residence without permission, curfew violation, entering restricted areas, associating with felons, and possession of firearms. Punitive policies contribute to prison growth as a self-perpetuating cycle.

There are promising in-prison and post-prison programs that are designed to help ex-convicts lead productive and crime-free lives. Community-based organizations, local businesses, and faith-based organizations, for example, have become important partners in assisting offenders with their transitions from prison to the community. Some states have been more progressive and have taken important first steps to effective offender reintegration. Rigorous scientific evaluation shows that such programs are reducing recidivism, as well as saving money and valuable community (and state/local) resources (Gelb & Velazquez, 2018). Recidivism in Georgia decreased 35% from 2007 to 2016 and 43% in Michigan from 2006 to 2015. In Virginia, the department of corrections attributed the state's low recidivism rate to policy makers' focus on reentry programming and treatment. Reducing recidivism lowers taxpayer spending on prisons, improves public safety, and helps formerly incarcerated people resume family and community responsibilities successfully.

Current practices in most states fail to reflect the evidence about what works; rather, false representations of crime and criminals, fear-mongering, and political posturing continue to be hallmarks of punitive practices. If our ultimate goal is a reduction in crime, then we must assess realistically what is needed for our offenders to succeed—this will translate into reduced crime, reduced victimization, and less human suffering (on both sides of the law).

> You were right. I finally met him [referring to a teacher in the education center], and it felt like the first time someone talked *to me* rather than *at me*. He counted me in as I came down earlier. He is such a delightful and compassionate man. You can see his heart in his eyes. I'm sure you know what I mean. He treats the women as human; he gives respect, and he is respected. It's unfortunate there are not more people like him working in the system. (personal communication)

> Guess who's going back to college? Me! You have to be tested, then the top 60 get in, if you're not in RDAP (the drug/alcohol treatment program) and if you have enough time (1 year)—which I do, duh! There are 3 classes, Business Office Specialist, Small Business Entrepreneurship, and Medical Transcribing and Coding. The last being the most sought after because it pays higher. So the 20 highest scores of the 60 get to choose 1st—yep, I got in! The grant is through Blinn College. I feel like I'm really doing something now with my wasted energy. Honestly, I'm close to the edge. This is going to be one of the hardest years of my life! Think about it . . . I spent the last 25 years destroying brain cells, now I'm going to have to work with what's left . . . wish me luck! (personal communication)

Over 600,000 people transition from incarceration to the community each year (Couloute & Kopf, 2018). Prisoner reentry has emerged as a key policy issue, but not just because of its impact on crime. Direct consequences of crime are imprisonment, fines, and community supervision. There are also collateral consequences that those who have been convicted of a crime confront as they attempt to develop productive lives after release (Forrest, 2016). Collateral effects move beyond the offender and the prison and include crucial social, political, and economic consequences for families and entire communities.

Only 2 states (Maine and Vermont) impose no restriction on voting by citizens convicted of felony offenses; 6.1 million Americans are prohibited from voting due to disenfranchisement laws (Chung, 2019). The 12 most extreme states restrict voting rights even after the person serves his or her sentence and is no longer on probation or parole. Over half the disenfranchisement population lives in those states. Disenfranchisement policies have a disproportionate impact on communities of color. African Americans are more than 4 times as likely to lose their voting rights then the rest of the adult population; 1 in 13 black adults is disenfranchised—2.2 million African American citizens are banned from voting.

Beyond voting rights and restrictions on owning firearms, there are thousands of other consequences of conviction that vary by jurisdiction and duration (Forrest, 2016). Offenders facing reentry may not be eligible for certain types of employment, may be barred from public housing, and may not be allowed to reunite with a child. The American Bar Association conducted a national study compiling collateral consequences for federal and state criminal convictions. The results of the study are available on an interactive website, the National Inventory of the Collateral Consequences of Conviction. There are 45,000 collateral consequences and civil disabilities on the database. These restrictions can prevent people from obtaining loans, housing, higher education, and employment. The inventory also informs users about avenues to relief from civil disabilities, such as expungement.

The challenges of transitioning from prison to the community are numerous. Before the formerly incarcerated can learn new skills, find stable jobs, and address health problems, they need housing. The basic necessity of a home is often out of reach for the formerly incarcerated (Couloute & Kopf, 2018). Barriers to employment plus explicit discrimination have created a housing crisis that receives little attention. The formerly incarcerated are almost 10 times more likely to be homeless than the general population. Rates of homelessness are especially high for people recently released from prison, people who have been incarcerated more than once, and people of color and women. Being homeless increases the risk of being arrested and incarcerated again because of policies that criminalize homelessness. Law enforcement agencies enforce offenses such as sleeping in public spaces, panhandling, and public urination, funneling the formerly incarcerated into the revolving door of incarceration. Stable housing is the foundation of successful reentry.

Over the years, the U.S. has passed many laws restricting the kinds of jobs for which an ex-offender can be hired. The unemployment rate for the formerly incarcerated is more than 27%—5 times higher than among the general public and higher than the unemployment rate during any historical period including the Great Depression (Couloute & Kopf, 2018). The unemployment rate for formerly incarcerated African American women is 43.6% compared to 23.2% for formerly incarcerated white women. Unemployment is highest (31.6%) within the first 2 years of release. The counterproductive system of release and poverty hurts the formerly incarcerated, employers, and taxpayers.

Females in the criminal justice system likely suffer a greater income-related burden from criminal conviction than do men (Hersch & Meyers, 2019). After release, most women prisoners will have no one to depend on but themselves. They must find a job that will provide income and advancement. The process is even more difficult given that women typically pursue jobs that require occupational licensing. Felony convictions often prohibit an individual from obtaining licensure. There are a number of laws that restrict an ex-offender's ability to obtain employment by limiting access to occupational licenses and certifications on the basis of a criminal record, either automatically or at the discretion of the employer. In all states, those practicing cosmetology are required to be licensed by the state, and most or all states restrict licensing for ex-offenders. "Interestingly, Pennsylvania requires candidates for cosmetology licenses to be of good moral character, although there is no such requirement for barbers" (p. 184).

Many of the women I met were the sole caregiver in their families prior to arrest. Without means of support, they face lives dependent on welfare or illegal activities to fulfill their children's needs and her own. There are far fewer vocational programming opportunities in prison for women. Programs to train offenders for post-release jobs, as well as incentives to pursue new opportunities, are essential if offenders are to succeed in the community. Finding suitable housing and employment are key factors in their success.

Even before I was convicted or had served any time, I had an extraordinarily difficult time finding a job. I appealed my sentence in early 2004 and was allowed to remain free until an appeal decision was made. I was monitored and under community supervision. I resigned my university teaching position at the end of the spring semester and tried to decide what I would do next. I needed financial support, so my first efforts went to searching for a job. I also knew that I needed to find a new, far less expensive place to live. The pursuit of employment was an incredibly frustrating and embarrassing process, and far more difficult than I would have predicted. I had a PhD, no prior criminal record, substantial ties to the community, family support, a nice place to live, and I had a stable home life. Despite *all* of these things, few businesses would even consider my application, much less take the time to meet with me or discuss my criminal background. I filled out close to 30 job applications—everything from hotel housecleaning, coffee shops, retail stores, dry cleaning businesses, bookstores, restaurants, learning centers for young people struggling in school, as well as a number of others. I even began to "dumb-down" my resume and my experiences; I changed the way I looked, dressed, and talked. I clearly remember the feelings of insignificance and worthlessness that began to take root. I ultimately ended up working in a roadside Farmers Market, and I'm fairly certain the only reason I was hired was because they were desperate for help. I started *that* day, my first minimum wage job since high school. One of the women made the following statement regarding her post-prison possibilities.

> I am truly blessed by such a loving husband and family. Like your situation with your brother, my relationship with my sister and brother have been strengthened by this journey. My marriage is stronger than it's even been. My appreciation for my friends and family has greatly increased. I can't ever imagine taking that for granted again. I know that it won't be easy to find a job, but I also know that my family loves me, and they forgave me a long time ago—and

that is a truly wonderful thing to go home too. A rarity with many in prison I'm afraid. (personal communication)

THE HELP WE NEED TO SUCCEED

While there was some political support for criminal justice reform efforts to slow our mass incarceration binge and ease the burden of community reentry for offenders, these efforts had only marginal impacts (Kelly, 2016). Reform efforts such as rolling back some mandatory sentences and banning the box (the requirement to disclose past criminal justice involvement on employment and academic applications) are modifications to the justice system that could have real and positive outcomes on recidivism rates.

Reentering offenders could also be helped by expanding community resources to include more treatment offerings for drug abuse and mental health care for those with no insurance. Offenders who need to remain on a particular medication, for example, or maintain a variety of medical treatments, are ill-equipped to pay for the services after release. Most offenders do not have insurance. As discussed above, they are unlikely to find post-prison employment that will provide a sufficient income to pay for necessary services. Prior to incarceration, a significant number of women were forced to choose between important medications (for themselves or other family members) or providing food and utilities for their children. The offender often lacks any sort of community support; they don't know how to ask for help or where to go to find it.

There is a crucial intersection between poverty and crime, the criminalization of mental illness, and the devastating effects of war on drugs. The health, welfare, and social needs of female inmates (and indeed male prisoners as well) are not being met prior to incarceration and are rarely improved while they are locked up. A prison sentence does not erase the serious issues that inmates bring with them into prison. Substance abuse, mental health issues, family fragmentation, economic instability, residential mobility, and social isolation have insurmountable effects on women in the criminal justice system. The lack of effectiveness with current correctional practices can be seen in the high rate of recidivism among young women, many of whom are sole supporters of their children.

The President's Commission (1969) more than fifty years ago found that the offender in prison was likely to be a member of the lowest social and economic groups in the country. This finding remains true today. FCI Tallahassee was not unique in the demographics of its female prisoners, particularly regarding the socioeconomic status of the majority of the women. Correctional facilities all across the country can be seen as "national poorhouses." U.S. prisons and jails predominantly confine the poor—not because these are the people most likely to harm us. Rather, the criminal justice system effectively weeds out the more affluent, so that the vast majority of those we find locked up come from the lower classes.

The U.S. Department of Housing and Urban Development (HUD) has recently put landlords and other housing providers on notice that a policy of denying housing to anyone with a prior arrest or any kind of criminal conviction would violate the Fair Housing Act. This Act prohibits racial discrimination in the sale, rental, or financing of homes. A policy refusing to rent or sell homes to people who have criminal records is illegal discrimination. Research suggests that 600,000 people released from prisons each year face a housing crisis (Couloute, 2018). It makes sense that formerly incarcerated people, legally and financially excluded from safe and affordable housing, will have substantial difficulties reintegrating successfully back into their communities.

There are some practical efforts being made to assist ex-offenders who, by virtue of the criminal status, will most likely be housing insecure as they transition from incarceration to the community. In New York City, for example, more than 54% of people released from prison moved straight into the city's shelter in 2017. If people don't have stable housing when they get out, they're much more likely to recidivate. In Washington State, the Tacoma Housing Authority provides rental assistance to formerly incarcerated college students at risk of homelessness. The Georgia Department of Corrections opened a transitional state prison (Metro Reentry Facility) for inmates scheduled for release within 18 months (Wiltz, 2019). Offenders returning to the community receive intensive counseling, vocational training, and housing support. One of the goals is that no one is released to homelessness.

The Second Chance Act (SCA) supports state, local, and tribal governments and nonprofit organizations in their work to reduce recidivism and improve outcomes for people returning from prisons, jails, and juvenile facilities. It was signed into law on April 9, 2008. The First Step Act was enacted in December 2018. It reauthorizes the Second Chance Act and will help reform the federal prison system by making significant changes to federal sentencing laws, as well as improvements to programs that aim to support people who are involved in the justice system. Of specific importance to women in prison, the First Step legislation puts an end to the shackling of pregnant women and restrictions on access to menstrual hygiene products.

> I am finally getting transferred up to Lexington, at least now I'll be near my friends and family. I'm hoping to get even closer to home by getting to the halfway house (since the Second Chance Law passage allows for a year), I realize that there are many more women who need that service and time more than I do, so I am grateful that I will be getting the 6 months. I am so thrilled and also anxious. I know you understand that. Even though it hasn't been that long, I am filled with anxiety wondering whether I will be able to find a job . . . I'm anxious thinking that everyone will know all my history . . . or worse, that somehow I will break some cardinal rule by not telling everyone what happened. I want to try and get one count expunged (the legal folks I've talked to here seem to think that's possible). I want to do that, but (again) I am afraid of causing myself more problems. Getting out is hard enough. But I know you understand . . . once you've been in this place, you worry that you'll never be yourself anywhere else. I tend to think of it like being in a nursing home. I can recall picking my grandmother up from the nursing home because she so badly wanted me to come and get her and take her somewhere. But as soon as we left the nursing home, she wanted to go back. Although it wasn't home, she had grown accustomed to the dysfunctional nature of its environment . . . such that she felt strange anyplace else. I know you get that because we've talked about it. (personal communication)

ACADEMIC BARRIERS AND STUDENT MENTORING

A criminal record attaches to a person permanently, and it is the instrument that allows for countless forms of legalized discrimination. These collateral consequences persist long after a woman completes her sentence. As mentioned, a criminal record affects employment, occupational licensing, housing, welfare benefits, voting rights, and parental rights (to name a few). Additionally, there are substantial barriers for those individuals seeking to improve their education, as there are a wide range of laws and institutional policies that target college students who have previous involvement in the criminal justice system. Three national surveys of post-secondary institutions conducted by separate research teams found that 60 to 80% of private institutions and 55% of public institutions collect criminal justice information for all prospective students (Scott-Clayton, 2017). If individuals with a criminal record decide to attend college, they are likely to face substantial challenges. I have advised a significant number of these students—sometimes the advice is academic-related, other times it's more personal. The one constant is that students often do not complete their college application forms once they realize they have to disclose their criminal backgrounds.

It makes sense that a university would want to be aware of individuals who committed violent crimes, or crimes against children, but all of the students I have counseled over the years were convicted of nonviolent and/or drug related crimes. Campus administrators argue that criminal history policies are necessary to keep campuses safe; however, the limited research available does not support this institutional perspective (Scott-Clayton, 2017). Significant research does support the fact that increased access to education decreases subsequent criminal behavior.

I continue to use my personal experiences in the academic and employment markets as a platform for change in my community and with my university. Recently, I went to our admissions department to ask about auditing an online course. After completing my initial application, the office staff member leaned in closely and whispered, "You checked yes in the crime box, did you mean to do that?" She actually appeared embarrassed *for me*. Fortunately, I have grown relatively comfortable in my ex-offender skin, and I answered her with an audible and assertive "Yes, I intentionally 'checked the box.'" These are the awkward and embarrassing moments I share with students, hoping to combat stereotyping by promoting empathy. In June 2017, Louisiana became the first state to ban all public colleges in the state from asking about criminal history in the application process, with exceptions for convictions related to sexual assault or stalking (Roll, 2017).

In an effort to bring awareness to the struggles posed for students with criminal histories (for both potential students and those currently enrolled), I have had a number of conversations with university administrators suggesting alternatives to a one-size-fits-all admissions background check. Understandably, there needs to be a balance between university safety and the rights of someone wanting to obtain post-secondary education, and that can be difficult. I believe college applications should avoid overly broad inquiries about criminal history. The questioning should also include specific time limits on the criminal background. Students I have spoken with describe crimes committed 5, 10, or even 20 years ago, and they wonder why they must still explain these. Another key distinction that should be made in the college application has to do with inquiring about *convictions*, rather than *arrests*—these are two very distinct terms with very different outcomes and should not be bundled into one admission question. One final suggestion might be to tailor criminal history questions to avoid unnecessarily precluding applicants from entering training programs (and thus employment).

One of the many ways my prison experience impacts me has to do with my role as a teacher and student mentor. As mentioned at the beginning of this book, I do believe I am a better educator *because of* the fallout from the crime I committed. Having firsthand knowledge of the justice system—navigating the myriad judicial procedures and criminal justice personnel—in no way resembled the sterile, impartial, and equitable system portrayed in my graduate school studies. In its place, I found a fragmented, violent, and biased network concerned only with financial bottom lines, political ideology, and avoidance of personal accountability. As I began teaching again, I struggled with how to convey what I had learned to my students. I concede that there are many female offenders who do need to be incarcerated to keep the public safe. The challenge for me was asking my students to have compassion for offenders and to understand that we are not all the same. We deserve understanding and humane treatment.

I have discovered that I am a more outspoken, loyal, and fierce advocate for my students and for my community. The majority of my students, as well as those from other disciplines, are aware of my criminal background. With one or two exceptions, I have received tremendous support and respect from them. Students often come to me seeking advice about how to address their own experiences with the judicial system; they are worried about what their futures will hold. Several times a semester, students will ask me about acknowledging their criminal histories when applying for jobs, filling out student loan forms, or dealing with landlords who refuse to rent to them. The legal, correctional, and community responses *to me*—as a defendant, an inmate, and an ex-convict—left me hopeless, wounded, and voiceless. I work every day to improve these situations for students and for others who see a college education as a means to a better, crime-free life.

Being involved in my community has helped me combine my academic training with my negative institutional experiences. Over the last decade, I have volunteered with a variety of agencies focused on homelessness, domestic violence, offender reentry, and children of the incarcerated. I have learned a great deal from the people and places I have been lucky enough to be a part of, and I hope that giving back to my community can somehow make a difference. Ironically, there have been a number of occasions when my volunteer application was denied *because of* my criminal history. In these instances, I would follow up with the administrators in charge of these organizations, but rarely received an answer other than "that's our policy." It is this hypocrisy, seen in all aspects of the judicial system, that most frustrates me. I often wonder how different criminal justice reform might look if one were to ask an ex-convict. Similarly, how might prison release mechanisms (parole boards) be improved by including an ex-offender to lend insight and/or context into the details considered by decision-making committees? There is a positive, constructive role that ex-convicts could play in society. For most of us, however, our loss of rights, voices, and value extends far beyond our criminal sentences.

MY [RE]ENTRY

As I sat on the patio one morning thinking about how far I had actually fallen, of all the things I'd lost along the way, and worrying how I would ever get by after release, I recalled a conference presentation I had once attended. The speaker, a "non con" (someone who writes about prison conditions and experiences, but has never actually served time), was suggesting that the transition from prison to society *wasn't* that difficult, that if an individual had survived life in prison, there should be no reason survival in society couldn't be possible. He made it sound so effortless, as if the movement from one part of a convict's life to another was merely about physical location. As I sat on that cement stoop, it occurred to me that most of us can indeed survive prison, and that probably does mean we can survive life on the streets. But shouldn't there be more to life after prison than simple survival?

As a criminal and subsequent ex-con, when is my "debt" ever really paid? Can my proverbial criminal ledger ever be balanced? What would that look like? I wondered if I would ever be allowed to be angry at my situation. Should the stigma and shame associated with my journey through the system, or the pains beyond my imprisonment be enough? I wondered how "justice" would be measured and who would make that decision? I know I committed a crime, but when will my suffering be equivalent to that of the people I have hurt? And ultimately, how long will my "sentence" stretch beyond my actual period of incarceration?

> I'm glad you finally got an apartment—it was good that you had a friend help you out with signing the lease. That's bullshit that someone like you can't even find a decent place to live—what do you suppose that means for me? Fuck the furniture, you don't need any—less things to fall over when you're drunk. Plus, who needs the hassle of dusting everything. I say enjoy the emptiness. . . . A blow-up mattress should work well (I'm sure it's better than sleeping on the floor—especially for your old ass). Now all you need is a blow-up guy to keep you company on those long cold nights. (personal correspondence)

With the reduction in funding for educational services, vocational services, and/or recreational services within most facilities, incarceration has changed little about the offender's pre-prison existence. Victimization and/or brutalization in prison (which I saw and experienced firsthand), however, undoubtedly and tangibly changes the psyche and identity of the convict. We release people back to the same disadvantaged environments but with the added burden of a criminal label and the scars of the prison experience. When an offender recidivates, the justice system responds by punishing them with an *even longer* sentence—the absurdity of this logic baffles me.

> What the hell kind of job do you think I'm going to be able to find when I get out? I've been working in the warehouse, driving a forklift, I did the masonry program, hell, now that I'm at this place (she'd just been transferred to a new facility), I've started the medical transcription program. These are all good skills, don't get me wrong, but I'm also a convict. Me and some of the other girls think we should start a business mowing yards, landscaping, stuff like that—we'll call it "Lawns by Cons" (laughing)—what do you think? Fuck, if the school fires you after this book comes out, you can help run the business (laughing). (recent phone call)

Inmates typically get out of prison with little to no money; they often have no place to go; and most are required to pay outstanding court fees and/or restitution. If an offender is required to attend drug and/or alcohol treatment, she is often required to pay for it herself. As mentioned earlier, if offenders don't attend required treatment programs, or pay restitution/court fees, they can be written up for a technical violation. Depending on an individual's probation or parole officer, a violation may result in the offender's return to prison. Sadly, each year about 350,000 individuals return to jail or prison, often because of rule violations rather than new crimes (Pew Charitable Trusts, 2018).

> From 2007 to 2016, 37 states experienced simultaneous drops in their community corrections and crime rates. In many cases, these gains followed the adoption of evidence-based sentencing and corrections reforms that prioritized scarce supervision and treatment resources for higher-risk reduction programs and created incentives for compliance. (p. 2)

As I began the process of looking for a place to live following my incarceration, it became painfully clear that years of crime-free living were negated by one moment in time—30 plus years of giving to and working within my communities; paying taxes and living a "good" and spiritual life; numerous jobs working with high-risk children, the homeless, and the elderly;

an advanced education and teaching at a variety of schools meant nothing.

Setting up a residency is a complicated process for anyone—paying first and last month's rent, getting utilities hooked up, establishing accounts, etc. The process is even more challenging if one has very few financial resources. And a criminal background is an enormous impediment. In addition to my 6-month prison sentence, I was also on probation for the 5 years that followed. My first academic job out of prison required me to move across the country to Oregon. I drove there with nothing but a few suitcases and my two cats. I was thousands of dollars in debt, with no real idea of what the future would hold. My first attempt to rent an apartment was disappointing—I was denied because the apartment complex association thought I might be a high-risk tenant. I found another apartment and struggled with the honesty of filling out the application. Instead, a friend of mine agreed to fill it out for me—his name, his family's contact information, etc. Here I was breaking the law again, but I was so desperate to succeed. I lived in this two-bedroom apartment for a year, with nothing but a blow-up mattress and a curb-side table offered for free to anyone who would take it.

While in prison, a non-con friend of mine put me in touch with the Convict Criminology (CC) group. The key turning point for me came in the form of a letter from one of the founding members of the CC group. While typing that sentence, tears filled my eyes and I struggled to hold back my emotions. That evening in prison, for the first time since my ordeal began, I felt hope, and I felt as if I might finally breathe again. This "first generation" ensemble of amazing individuals extended a lifeline and showed me that second chances were possible. What we have done in the past is not necessarily who we are in the future. I owe much to this group and have worked hard to ease the burden the next generation of convicts will undoubtedly bear. Like many other women who have served time and are trying to find their way into higher education, I have an incredibly strong desire to bring about change and reform. It takes time, however, to heal, to set in motion a realistic plan for the future, and to reestablish (or to create for the first time) our support systems. Until this transition occurs, we remain quietly tucked into the folds of society. It took tenure for me to finally find my professional voice. Yet I still struggle with discussing my convict status with those around me.

My first post-prison academic position was difficult; I knew many of the other faculty did not want me there and in fact resented me. My time at the university was miserable, but I also spent that year getting to know the CC members, attending conferences, writing papers, and making presentations about my experiences. The weight of my future began to feel less and less oppressive. Through the nurturing friendships and academic camaraderie of the group, I found my way back to the profession I loved.

A year later I landed a full-time tenure track position in my current school, a program of which I am quite fond. But it has not been without its challenges. I have often been confronted about my felony conviction and subsequent incarceration. Interestingly enough, these confrontations have come from other faculty, not students. I have never officially "come out" at the school, but many were aware of my history. It felt dishonest to teach a corrections course or a theory course where we discussed the etiology of crime, violence, and sexual assault in prison, barriers to reentry, and the like without telling my students I had been convicted and incarcerated. I felt compelled to share my experiences with them, to put a white female face to the overwhelming male minority face of crime with which society is inundated. But at the urging of both my dean and my then department coordinator, I kept my convict status to myself. On some level, I knew they were right. Despite the appearance of a more liberal university environment, the reality was that my job was very much in constant danger. I focused on being the best teacher I could be. My reasoning was that if I had several years of solid teaching evaluations, steady and productive committee work, and the beginnings of a solid research agenda, I would be able to defend myself and my employment when I was "outed."

Most of my students now know about by criminal background, not because I have told them, but because they search the internet for information about their professors. Overall, the students seem far less concerned than the faculty—for some I am "cool." Others believe I have "earned" the right to be critical of the system and that my discussions mean *more* to them because I have lived the prison experience. Far more find comfort and a nonjudgmental shoulder as they themselves (their friends or family members) navigate the harsh, confusing, and unrelenting criminal justice machinery. It is in these moments, many of them quite personal, that I realize I have found the advocacy voice I discussed earlier. These daily student interactions and the connections with the women I mentor in my community make my convict experiences worthwhile. I know that I am lucky to have come so far, but I am also aware of the fragility of an academic career. As a result, I still guard my convict status closely.

Chapter Eleven

Beyond the Punishment

You need to see the dark in order to see the light.
—Bob Ross, painter

Even now, 15 years after my incarceration, I find myself consumed with the lives of the women I left behind. I am relieved and fortunate at where life has taken me, but I feel a deep sense of loss and guilt for those who remain caged, tucked neatly out of public sight. How strange it must sound to outsiders. We are, after all, merely criminals—too often defined as without feelings, lesser in spirit, and lacking in heart. I get phone calls periodically from some of the women in various facilities. On a good day (with no dropped or interrupted calls) the allotted 15 minutes fly by, and strangely it is as if I have been transported back in time. Very few people will understand how or why I look forward to these calls. Not only is it a chance to make sure the woman with whom I am talking is physically safe but it also, on a very personal level, allows me a brief moment in time when it is OK to be an ex-con. I have amazing friends and family who have been nothing but loving and supportive. Yet, those all-too-rare 15 minutes are when my walls can come down completely—and that place in my soul that I work so hard to hide opens up. It is both painful and liberating. For that brief period in time, I am completely exposed, and yet I feel more at ease in those moments than most others in my day. I cannot explain it, nor do I really want to try. It just is, and I long for those times more than I particularly care to admit.

> You once said that even though you are now "home," you feel a different kind of comfort when you're around ex-offenders. I think it's true . . . and maybe it's because at a

time when we are most vulnerable, we are forced to share a space and time with strangers. And if we are lucky, they treat us as family, and at the very least, as friends brand new. (personal communication)

We both know that the women here live in us . . . no matter how much we may want or think differently. We can't forget them, nor should we. We may put this behind us, but there is a reason that it stays within us . . . so that we are more compassionate, more considerate, and more forgiving of others. I've said it often—I would never have chosen this road, but it has been a good road, and I am forever blessed to have walked it. (personal communication)

In addition to the hopelessness, pain, and desperation, I also witnessed genuine companionship, unmatched by anything I had experienced in my life. There are times now that I find I am far more comfortable in a room full of ex-cons than I am in a room full of academics or "professionals."

It seems to be a fairly familiar feeling among convicts that we tend to be more comfortable around other cons (or ex-cons). Perhaps it's the journey we share. You wondered if it was because you didn't have to hide anything from them (or that you wouldn't be judged as harshly) . . . and yet, I wonder if it is also that *they* are more at ease with *you*. Whether it's anyone's fault or not, I would expect a large part of the population in general is immediately fearful of anyone who has been in prison. I agree that most cannot possibly understand this environment or this "reality." A friend compared it to Vietnam Veterans. Rarely do they speak of war or their time in battle, except when they are with other veterans. When they are free to speak without offending or frightening someone, then they are more at ease to do so. They can speak of a similar experience. In that situation, neither has anything to fear, and in telling, they rid themselves of the ghosts that remain with them always. (personal communication)

I watched friendships grow in women who had spent the majority of their lives equating love with pain and suffering. I endured violence, fear, and trepidation almost daily. But I need to let the reader know that I also experienced friendship, laughter, camaraderie, and a sense of belonging. I recall a number of evenings spent sitting outside on "the patio," talking with the women about life, love, goals and aspirations, fear, grief, and loss. We could have been anywhere. Sitting with one or two of the women I have come to call friends reminded me of the power of faith and the value of self-reflection. Most of us would never have been friends in any other world; we were friends now by virtue of a shared criminality. I met strong and gifted women devoted to their families, blessed in their friendships with others, and humbled by the grace of God. I met women who'd spent years being battered and beaten. While I did meet women from power, wealth, and money, the majority of women struggled against abuse, poverty, limited resources, and a dismal outlook for the future. Many of these women are uneducated, but not stupid. They are tired; they are out of hope, love, and opportunities. They have simply given up on a society that gave up on them a long time ago.

> Behind these walls are some of the most beautiful women I have ever seen—elegant, demur, proud, and even stunning. Unfortunately, most of the women around me, although they try to hide it, project a look of death and desperation. The effects of drugs and alcohol are vividly clear. Their bodies and their minds are marked by permanent stains of abuse. The vacant look in their eyes and the stories they tell haunt me. (journal entry)

> As I look back on my 6 months (being released tomorrow) I wonder where my time went. It makes P.'s remaining 10 months and T.'s year "do-able." I'm hoping L. gets her sentence reduction and gets back to family in Texas. And I hope the other L. gets through the next few years, or at the very least, back to DC where she can be close to her family. If someone would have told me I would not only make friends in prison, but that I would come to care about convicts I met along the way, I would have said they were crazy. But that is exactly what happened. These women are far more than common criminals, even if they don't believe it themselves. (journal entry)

> It's so loud in here tonight because [a certain female guard] is working and she's just as mean and obnoxious as the women. We see her at 4 p.m. count and 10 p.m. count, but never in between. The women run wild all night because she's too busy sitting in the front office talking with her "friends." I know I won't miss all of this chaos . . . my cube mates are funny tonight though . . . I will miss them a bit. How is it I feel guilty for leaving these women behind? M. is

getting a pedicure, T. is working with one of the Spanish mommies on her English, and S. has sort-of just floated amongst a number of her friends. L. (next door) is in typical fashion, sitting on her bunk quietly reading, pictures of her kids spread out in front of her. She chimes into various conversations now and then. I will miss her singing to me (and others) at night . . . it's peaceful and soothing. I know I have been one of the lucky ones with regards to my bunkies. We got on each other's nerves on occasion, but when it counted, we were there for each other, standing together against both convict and guard. (journal entry, last night in prison)

Very little was respected among the women, but I observed a strange sanctity in the memories and reminders of loved ones—children, husbands, life-partners. Even the "enemies" could come together in shared celebration of family. There was a primacy in these relationships, and this had an enormous impact on the overall values shaping the culture of the facility. Milestones such as birthdays and anniversaries were acknowledged with warmth and respect, but also with grief and intensity. Tragedy was all around us—some from far-off places, others from a bunk or two over. Several women died while I was there. How or why they died matters little now, but the way the women came together to express anger, hopelessness, and desperation demonstrated a group cohesion that was rarely seen.

I had several bunkmates while I was locked up, but T. was my favorite! She was lovely! She was a young, cherub-faced, heavy-set, single mother, with a fantastic sense of humor, and an unnerving grasp on the bleak life that would exist for her after release. In the dark wee hours of the night, while some women slept, and some engaged in intimate relations, we would lay in our bunks mourning for the lives we thought we deserved to live. We would nibble on ill-gotten packs of dry *Top Ramen*, or we would share pop-tarts acquired earlier in the day. And while wine (prison "hooch") was available from time to time, she would giggle and remind me that *"we were on the wagon."* I enjoyed her company very much. We talked often of her pain, just below the surface of her infectious smile and clever wit. She was an addict—any drug would do (she often told me); she had at least one diagnosable mental illness, and a long and very sad history of violent physical and sexual abuse. Despite her pain, she was always so positive and upbeat. I could not help but feel ashamed of myself for wallowing in self-pity. T. was not stupid. She was painfully aware of what life would most likely hold for her following prison, but she seemed to take each day with hopeful and welcoming vision. She knew her odds for success were not good, but she wanted to do more than survive. She served another year and half after I left. We wrote and spoke several times, but I have since lost track of her. I miss her and worry what might have become of her.

> Another day, another chance. New hope, new mercy. [Writing on a bathroom stall.]

> I am so fucked up! I think the really exhausting part is trying to maintain the way I feel on the inside while projecting an entirely different image on the outside. It's amazing what has stuck with me from inside to out—I still sleep with a shirt over my eyes and on occasion, I sleep with my radio headset on. I'm afraid of the dark (still), but somehow the dark with the shirt over my eyes is less scary than the dark I cannot reach out and touch. I have joked about making a tape of jingling keys or having flashlight strobe-effect night lights—it's crazy the things you get used to. (journal entry following release)

I noticed a number of strange "leaving" ceremonies or behaviors, especially from those women with exceptionally long sentences, almost as if they lived vicariously through people leaving. It is understandably difficult for these women, whether they have just started a lengthy sentence, or have already served a substantial amount of time. Both groups seem to go through a "grieving" (for lack of a better word) process. It is really sad, and it makes my heart hurt to watch them go through it and to see the hopelessness in their eyes. Their conversations are a strange combination of joy for those getting out, and an undercurrent of envy. I hated prison. I hated most of the women there. And yet, I cry for them and the lives they'll never live.

The "justice" system is rife with fragmentation and inconsistencies; the resulting disorientation ultimately leads to gross misunderstanding, ill-suited responses, biases, and abuse. We have labeled it the field of "corrections." However, very little correcting takes place. We have developed processes to facilitate offender "reentry," while most offenders were never *entered into* society in the first place. To fund and build programs based on this notion is to create a reality based on fiction. I am not suggesting these issues should be abandoned, but it appears that it is the perception of others that becomes a prisoner's reality. Many scholars and practitioners (even teachers), appear more comfortable looking at and writing about officially processed data, rather than talking to a convict (or even a victim).

Political schemas are set by data culled from "like-minded" sources and elections fueled by distortions and fear. Much of what I have read and studied over the last few years reeks of individual vision, ideology, and agenda rather than the real lives and personal experiences of the people who have lived it. Those of us who are former prisoners turned teachers (or political consultants or legal experts) are not claiming that our experiences necessarily make us better criminologists. Rather, we emphasize that someone can know what something is yet not really understand the ramifications of living it.

> It seems like all my life I have been in search of something and that is one reason I allowed myself to fall into drugs and my abuse. It is sad to say that I have not found much confidence since coming to prison. I think I'd like to go back to school, but let's face it, I'm not that smart! I do want to better myself economically and mentally. My achievements in life have been few, you know that, but the ones I've had felt good! I want to be independent and to have basic things I can call my own and to take care of my children and family. I am determined to break the cycle of being poor and the abuse that has been passed down in my family. (personal communication)

There is no denying the fact that the United States leads the world in producing prisoners, a reflection of a relatively recent and idiosyncratic approach to crime and punishment. People in our nation's jails and prisons are demonized by a society that seems to pride itself on being enlightened, informed, and educated. The damage done to women, men, and children in and around the justice system suggests this is not the case. People are locked up for crimes ranging from writing bad checks to using drugs—crimes that would rarely produce prison sentences in other countries. In addition, sentences to incarceration are far longer than sentences in other nations. Our system is broken and flawed. Much of our judicial sentencing ignores of the many social ills that typically precede and foster criminal activity. The processes and unending formalities create a veneer of fairness and justice. Degradation and abuse are justified in the name of safety and security. Our system hides the truth, much like it hides its criminals.

The U.S. incarceration rate (860 per 100,000) was the lowest in 20 years in 2016 (Kaeble & Cowhig, 2018). However, more than 1.5 million people were in prison, almost 750,000 people were in jail, more than 3.6 million people were on probation, and almost 875,000 were on parole. About 1 in 38 adults were under some form of correctional supervision. Violent crime rates and property crime rates have declined steadily since the early 1990s (Kappeler & Potter, 2018). Despite reduced crime rates, the number of people incarcerated in prisons and jails increased through 2008. Many incarcerated offenders committed misdemeanors or minor drug offenses. The following comments illustrate society's tendency to throw people away.

> I am a 27-year old Black woman with 3 children. I am a first-time offender and innocent of crime . . . just guilty of association with my child's father. I have served 9 years of a life sentence.

> I have been locked up for 5 years, I have 27 more years to go. I was charged with conspiracy for selling coke. All of my co-defendants turned on me for plea bargains, but I trusted the system and went to trial. I will be almost 70 when I get out—what kind of life will have I then?

Most people have no concept of what it means to "do time." Prisons, for both men and women, are seen as obscure and distant places of punishment and deterrence where pain and suffering are allowed and at times even encouraged.

Common thought has it that the prison system is not so bad, and that prison time is easy or inconsequential. Prisons today are indeed far less cruel than when they were first invented, but that does not mean that incarceration is an experience without pain. In place of physical suffering, the modern prison inflicts a far more severe damage that is spiritual and social in nature. The loss of freedom is indeed fundamental, as is the loss of social status and the lifetime of labeling that come with being a convict.

Chuck Terry (2000) proffers that in addition to the physical adjustment to isolation in an overcrowded and often violent world, there is a psychological adjustment that must be made as well. The problem is not simply being locked up with hundreds of strangers, but with the difficulty of having one's self-esteem and identity inundated with the evidence of an unsuccessful life and the view that you are somehow less human and less worthy. Few see prison as an intricate social and psychological world, where the individual is extraordinarily overwhelmed and hampered with challenges so profound that one's identity is at stake. There is a self-loathing that develops among convicts (myself included), a personal feeling of diminished self-worth perpetuated by a system more concerned with effectiveness and efficiency than with human life.

> I feel lost . . . how crazy is that? I also feel guilty that I am out here, and they are still in there. I was in prison for 6 months, 6 months of hell, the lowest point in my life ever. I was down only a short time and I cannot even pretend that I know what it's like to serve a lengthy sentence. But even with my short sentence, there is a hole left in my soul and it feels like it can only be filled by those people who understand the damage that is done, the anger that creeps in, the idiosyncrasies that are acquired, and the dreams I cannot escape. (journal entry 13 days after release)

beginning again
if given the words
could write you a story
and spin you a truth
of lies I know well
ten thousand excuses
not one worth repeating
would you dare remember
the choice I could tell
this place is my doing
my fate still becoming
when blinded by want
beyond mine to touch
so easy to see
now
the way I neglected
a lifetime of blessings
a moment too much
what price I would pay
to change then the future
to relive every second
my will to concede
to right every wrong
of this journey returning
life filled with purposes
this destiny seed
but now I must go
only one way is waiting
back to the light
I betrayed my youth
back to the giver
of life everlasting
beginning again
my story of truth
bw

(personal communication)

References

The Annie E. Casey Foundation. (2016, April 18). A shared sentence: The devastating toll of parental incarceration on kids, families, and communities.

Arditti, J. (2012). *Parental incarceration and the family: Psychological and social effects of imprisonment on children, parents, and caregivers*. New York: NYU Press.

Austin, J., & Irwin, J. (2012). *It's about time: America's imprisonment binge* (4th ed.). Belmont, CA: Wadsworth.

Bandele, M. (2017, October 23). Here's how prison and jail systems brutalize women, especially mothers. ACLU.

Beck, A. J., Berzofsky, M., Caspar, R., & Krebs, C. (2013). Sexual victimization in prisons and jails reported by inmates 2011–2012. Washington DC: Bureau of Justice Statistics. NCJ 241399.

Bronson, J., & Carson, E. A. (2019, April). Prisoners in 2017. Washington DC: Bureau of Justice Statistics. NCJ 252156.

Bruenig, E. S. (2015, March 2). Why Americans don't care about prison rape. *The Nation*.

Bureau of Justice Statistics. (2018, June). PREA data collection activities, 2018. Washington, DC: Bureau of Justice Statistics. NCJ 251672.

Celinska, K., & Sung, H. (2014). Gender differences in the determinants of prison rule violations. *The Prison Journal*, 94(2), 220–241.

Chen, M. (2018, May 29). By 2030, 1 in 3 US prisoners will be over 50. *The Nation*.

Chiu, T. (2010). It's about time: Aging prisoners, increasing costs, and geriatric release. New York: Vera Institute of Justice.

Chung, J. (2019, June 27). Felony disenfranchisement: A primer. The Sentencing Project.

Clarke, M. (2007, August 15). Six Florida federal prison guards convicted, sentenced on rape and corruption charges. *Prison Legal News*.

Clear, T. R. (1994). *Harm in American penology: Offenders, victims, and their communities*. Albany: State University of New York Press.

Clear, T. R. (2007). *Imprisoning communities: How mass incarceration makes disadvantaged neighborhoods worse*. New York: Oxford University Press.

Clear, T. R., & Frost, N. A. (2014). *The punishment imperative: The rise and failure of mass incarceration in America.* New York: New York University Press.

Clear, T. R., Reisig, M. D., & Cole, G. F. (2019). *American corrections* (12th ed.). Boston: Cengage.

Couloute, L. (2018, August). Nowhere to go: Homelessness among formerly incarcerated people. Prison Policy Initiative.

Couloute, L., & Kopf, D. (2018, July). Out of prison & out of work: Unemployment among formerly incarcerated people. Prison Policy Initiative.

Currie, E. (2013). *Crime and punishment in America* (rev. and updated). New York: Picador.

Editorial. (2019, July 22). Illinois prison strip searches and the Constitution. *Chicago Tribune,* p. 13.

Eisen, L. (2015, May 21). Charging inmates perpetuates mass incarceration. The Brennan Center for Justice.

Endicott, M. (2018, August 29). No longer human: Women's prisons are a breeding ground for sexual harassment, abuse. ThinkProgress.

Evans, D. N. (2014, August 15). The debt penalty: Exposing the financial barriers to offender reintegration. Research and Evaluation Center, John Jay College of Criminal Justice.

Federal Bureau of Prisons. (2019). Southeast Regional Office. Retrieved from https://www.bop.gov/locations/regional_offices/sero/

Forrest, C. E. (2016). Collateral consequences of a criminal conviction: Impact on corrections and reentry. *Corrections Today,* 30–31.

Friedmann, A. (2014, October 10). How courts view ACA accreditation. *Prison Legal News.*

Gelb, A., & Valazquez, T. (2018, August 1). The changing state of recidivism: Fewer people going back to prison. PEW Trusts.

Hager, E., & Flagg, A. (2018, December 2). How incarcerated parents are losing their children forever. The Marshall Project.

Harding, D. J., Morenoff, J. D., Nguyen, A. P., & Bushway, S. D. (2017, October). Short- and long-term effects of imprisonment on future felony convictions and prison admissions. *Proceedings of the National Academy of Sciences, 114*(42), 11103–11108. doi:170154414

Hassine, V. (2011). *Life without parole: Living and dying in prison today* (5th ed.). New York: Oxford University Press.

Hersch, J., & Myers, E. (2019). The gendered burdens of conviction and collateral consequences on employment. *Notre Dame Journal of Legislation, 45*(2), 171–193.

Incarcerated Workers Organizing Committee. (2018, June 12). Prison strike 2018: History and endorsement from the fire inside collective.

Irwin, J. (1980). *Prisons in turmoil.* Boston: Little, Brown.

Jefferson, R. (2018, May 25). Should older prisoners get a pass just because they're old? *Forbes.*

Kaeble, D., & Cowhig, M. (2018). Correctional populations in the United States, 2016. Washington, DC: Bureau of Justice Statistics, NCJ 251211.

Kajstura, A. (2018, November). Women's mass incarceration: The whole pie 2018. Prison Policy Initiative.

Kappeler, V., & Potter, G. (2018). *The mythology of crime and criminal justice* (5th ed.). Long Grove, IL: Waveland Press.

Kelly, W. R. (2016). *The future of crime and punishment: Smart policies for reducing crime and saving money.* Lanham, MD: Rowman & Littlefield.

Kreager, D., & Kruttschnitt, C. (2018). Inmate society in the age of mass incarceration. *Annual Review of Criminology, 1,* 261–283.

Krisberg, B., Marchionna, S., & Hartney, C. (2015). *American corrections: Concepts and controversies.* Thousand Oaks, CA: Sage.

Law, V. (2019, May 21). When abuse victims commit crimes. *The Atlantic.*

Leonard, N. (2017, November 21). Will the prison rape epidemic ever have its Weinstein moment? *The Intercept.*

Mallicoat, S. L. (2018). *Women, gender, and crime: Core concepts.* Thousand Oaks, CA: Sage.

Owen, B. A. (1998). *In the mix: Struggle and survival in a women's prison.* Albany: State University of New York Press.

Owen, B. A., Wells, J., & Pollock, J. M. (2017). *In search of safety: Confronting inequality in women's imprisonment.* Oakland: University of California Press.

Pew Charitable Trusts. (2018, September 25). Probation and parole systems marked by high stakes, missed opportunities. PEW Research.

Pollock, J. M. (2014). *Women's crimes, criminology, and corrections.* Long Grove, IL: Waveland Press.

President's Commission on Law Enforcement and Administration of Justice. (1967, February). The challenge of crime in a free society. Washington DC: Government Printing Office.

Rabuy, B., & Kopf, D. (July, 2015). Prisons of poverty: Uncovering the pre-incarceration incomes for the imprisoned. Northampton, MA: Prison Policy Initiative.

Rabuy, B. & Kopf, D. (May, 2016). Detaining the poor: How the money bail perpetuates an endless cycle of poverty and jail time. Prison Policy Initiative.

Raher, S. (May, 2018). The company store: A deeper look at prison commissaries. Prison Policy Initiative.

Rantala, R. (2018, July). Sexual victimization reported by adult correctional authorities, 2012–15. Washington, DC: Bureau of Justice Statistics. NCJ 251146.

Reiman, J. & Leighton, P. (2017). *The rich get richer and the poor get prison: Ideology, class, and criminal justice* (11th ed.). New York: Routledge.

Roll, N. (2017, June 19). Louisiana becomes the first state to ban the box. Inside Higher Ed.

Ross, J. I., & Richards, S. C. (2003). *Convict criminology.* Belmont, CA: Wadsworth.

Santo, A. (2017, October 10). What is prison like for women and girls? The Marshall Project.

Santo, A. (2018, July 25). Prison rape allegations are on the rise. The Marshall Project.

Sawyer, W. (2018, January 9). The gender divide: Tracking women's state prison growth. Prison Policy Initiative.

Sawyer, W. (2019, July 19). Who's helping the 1.9 million women released from prisons and jails each year? Prison Policy Initiative.

Sawyer, W., & Wagner, P. (2019, March 19.). Mass incarceration: The whole pie. Prison Policy Initiative.

Scott-Clayton, J. (2017, September 28). Thinking "beyond the box": The use of criminal records in college admissions. The Brookings Institution.

The Sentencing Project. (2019, June). Incarcerated women and girls.

Shapiro, J., Pupovac, J., & Lydersen, K. (2018, October 15). In prison, discipline comes down hardest on women. National Public Radio.

Shelden, R., Brown, W., Miller, K., & Fritzler, R. (2016). *Crime and criminal justice in American society* (2nd ed.). Long Grove, IL: Waveland Press.

Shelden, R., & Vasiliev, P. (2018). *Controlling the dangerous classes: A history of criminal justice in America* (3rd ed.). Long Grove, IL: Waveland Press.

Shelden, R., and Veléz, M. (2020). *Our punitive society* (2nd ed.). Long Grove, IL: Waveland Press.

Silber, R., Shames, A., & Reid, K. (2017, December). Aging out: Using compassionate release to address the growth of aging and infirm prison populations. New York: Vera Institute of Justice.

Smith, S. (2017). Women and girls in the justice system. Williamsburg, VA: National Center for State Courts.

Stannow, L. (2017, November 7). Op-ed: What's life like for thousands of incarcerated women? *Los Angeles Times*.

Stohr, M. K., Jonson, C.O., & Lux, J. L. (2015). Understanding the female prison experience. In F. T. Cullen, P. Wilcox, J. L Lux, & C. L. Jonson (Eds.), *Sisters in crime revisited: Bringing gender into criminology* (pp. 351–370). New York: Oxford University Press.

Terry, C. M. (2000). Beyond punishment: Perpetuating difference from the prison experience. *Humanity and Society*, *24*(2), 108–135.

Trammell, R. (2009). Relational violence in women's prison: How women describe interpersonal violence and gender. *Journal of Women and Criminal Justice*, *19*(4), 267–285.

Trammell, R., Wulf-Ludden, T., & Mowder, D. (2015). Partner violence in women's prison: The social consequences of girlfriend fights. *Journal of Women and Criminal Justice*, *25*(4), 256–272.

Wagner, P. & Rabuy, B. (2017, January 25). Following the money of mass incarceration. Prison Policy Initiative.

Williams, M. (1991). *The velveteen rabbit*. New York: Doubleday; Reissue edition.

Wiltz, T. (2019, April 23). Cities try new ways to help former inmates find housing. GOVERNING.

Wooldredge, J., & Steiner, B. (2016). The exercise of power in prison organizations and implications for legitimacy. *Journal of Criminal Law and Criminology*, *106*(1), 125–165.

Index